TEACHER, PUPIL, AND TASK

Elements of Social Psychology
applied to Education

Teacher, Pupil, and Task

Elements of Social Psychology
applied to Education

A Practical Manual for Teachers
Edited by
O. A. OESER

SOCIAL SCIENCE PAPERBACKS
in association with
Tavistock Publications

First published in 1955
Second edition 1960
Reprinted 1965
First published in this series 1966
by Tavistock Publications Limited
Reprinted 1967
Reprinted 1970
Reproduced and printed in Great Britain
by Latimer Trend & Co. Ltd., Whitstable
SBN 422 72040 2
1·3

Distributed in the U.S.A. by
Barnes & Noble Inc.

Contents

                                                                    Page

Foreword by Maj-Gen. A. H. Ramsay,
    C.B., C.B.E., D.S.O., E.D., B.Sc., Dip.Ed.
    Director of Education, Victoria . . . ix

Preface xi

CHAPTER I. *O. A. Oeser.* *Society in Miniature: The Social Roles of Pupil and Teacher and their Relevance to the Acquisition of Knowledge* 1

A general introduction to the book. The social settings of the school and of the classroom. Social relations of the teacher. The functions of social relationships in the learning process. Roles and role discrepancies. Motivation and incentives. The problems of authority. The problems of establishing functional social links for the learning process and for general education in citizenship.

CHAPTER II. *E. R. Wyeth and W. C. Watson.* *The Teacher in the Educational Hierarchy; and the Teacher and the Curriculum* 17

How can permissive social climates be established if the headmaster were to insist upon a well-disciplined school in the traditional sense?
How can child-centred methods be established when a prescribed curriculum has to be followed?
Certain implications of these two questions are discussed.

CHAPTER III. *H. A. Presser, G. W. D. Boyd, and R. C. G. Lea.* *The Social Conditions for Successful Learning* . . 30

Since the problem of the nature and phases of motivation (Chapters 1 and 2) is so important, this chapter expands the argument. It aims to give the teacher a more thorough grasp of this topic before he attempts to appreciate and, later, to apply to classroom practice the methods of social psychology.

Contents

CHAPTER IV. *O. A. Oeser. The Classroom as a Social Group* . 50

The six types of psychological structure in the classroom. Their implications for different aspects and purposes of teaching.

CHAPTER V. *A. P. Ward. Sociometry* 64

Simple techniques by which the teacher can obtain a clear picture of the patterns of relationships which exist among the children of the class; examples from research and actual classroom situations which will help the teacher to interpret the data he obtains; practical use of these techniques in the classroom.

CHAPTER VI. *A. P. Ward and L. J. Murphy. Problems and Effects of Changing the Social Structure of the Classroom* 87

Some problems likely to be encountered when group methods are introduced for the first time. Criteria for assigning children to groups. Difficulties teachers meet under present conditions in the classroom. Specific suggestions about organizing group activities. Social implications of group work.

CHAPTER VII. *C. H. Doubay and G. Douglas. Psychological Tests and Testing* 105

Tests available to teachers are, broadly, of three kinds: tests of cognitive ability or 'intelligence', achievement and aptitude. Main attention in this chapter is given to the first two. It answers many questions about such tests and outlines what use can be made of test results for the more efficient organization of teaching and the benefit of individuals.

CHAPTER VIII. *F. L. Rouch. The Problem Child.* . . 124

Previous chapters have considered the need for classroom procedure which will enable the teacher to create and maintain a healthier spirit of peer group and teacher relations. Nevertheless, problems remain, partly because of physical or home conditions outside the teacher's control, partly because deviant behaviour has become so strong a habit that some special steps need to be taken to correct and restrain it. Aids for detecting cases in which individual, rather than group treatment becomes necessary. Types of cases. Appropriate action.

Contents

CHAPTER IX. *P. Lafitte and N. F. Holt. The Purpose and Conduct of Examinations* 144

> Evaluation is an important part of education. It is imperative that examinations be integrated with the process of teaching and learning, relevant to the content of teaching, and reliable. Advice to teachers on each of these points.

CHAPTER X. *A. R. Greig.   Educational and Vocational Guidance* 158

> Aspects of educational and vocational guidance with which the teacher should be concerned, and in which he can help his pupils to face and adjust to the problems and responsibilities of adult work roles.

Appendix. O. A. Oeser   181

> Outlines of a short theoretical and practical course in applied social psychology for teachers, which was based on this book.

Index   193

Foreword

By

MAJOR-GENERAL A. H. RAMSAY, C.B., C.B.E., D.S.O., E.D., B.Sc., Dip.Ed.

DIRECTOR OF EDUCATION, VICTORIA

THE first reaction of many teachers to a book on teaching written by psychologists will be to ask 'What do they know about teaching?' This question is easy to answer as far as this book is concerned.

About five years ago a Refresher School in Psychology was arranged by the Department of Psychology of the University of Melbourne at the request of the Refresher Schools Co-ordinating Committee, a body representative of the University and the State and Registered Schools. The method used in the Refresher School placed major emphasis on the use of discussion groups and relatively minor emphasis on lectures. Eleven of the group leaders were members of teachers' college staffs or of the psychology or research branches of the Education Department, and, as such, must be accepted as highly skilled practical teachers. No one is appointed to these staffs, however high his academic qualifications, unless he has proved himself as a successful teacher. Other group leaders were members of the University staff, most of whom had also had teaching experience in schools. The authors, then, can claim to be practical teachers, and the views expressed in this work have been hammered out in the discussions of some 250 teachers who participated in the discussion groups.

Foreword

The practice of any profession can never be static; new fields of knowledge are constantly being opened up, and this new knowledge must affect the current practices in medicine, in engineering, or in education. The difficulty in our own profession is to make teachers acquainted with the new knowledge, a task undertaken by the University, the teachers' colleges, and by our own psychology and research branches. Although staffing difficulties in our rapidly expanding schools have limited the numerical strength of these special branches, the quality of their personnel and of their work is very high. They are well qualified to give a lead to their fellow teachers.

This work deals with the application of social psychology to education. The growth of knowledge in this field of social psychology must have a bearing on practical teaching. How great will be the effect on our schools will depend on our ability to make the new knowledge available to teachers in a convenient and understandable form. There is no doubt that the 250 teachers who attended the Refresher School profited by their opportunity to meet those working in this special field and to discuss among themselves the implications of the new knowledge for them as teachers. The effect on their own attitude to their work and to the children they teach was most marked. The purpose of this book is to bring to all teachers help in gaining insight into the human problems faced daily by teachers.

The book is singularly free from the specialized technical vocabulary of the psychologist and provides both assistance and a challenge to the thoughtful teacher.

ALAN RAMSAY

11th October, 1954

Preface

Origin of the Book

IN May 1950 nearly three hundred teachers attended a three-day course at Melbourne University in the social psychology of classroom practice, a summary of which is given in Appendix I.

In this course, teaching was conducted through work in small discussion groups, with a minimum of formal lecturing and a maximum of 'pupil' participation. At the end, the participants demanded that a practical manual should be written to which they could refer. This volume is the response by the authors, who were the group leaders of the course, to that expressed need.

Should this volume find acceptance, the authors hope to follow it with a second, which will deal with the theoretical foundations of those parts of social psychology which can be applied directly to the practice of education.

Aim and Structure of the Book

Its aim is to give teachers an introduction to some of the considerations as well as techniques of psychology other than those which have to do with the details of learning a particular subject. The emphasis, therefore, is on social psychology and on developing the personality of the child. Furthermore, practice rather than theory is intended. Thus, there are no chapters on learning theory, personality, communication, level of aspiration, function pleasure, group structure and dynamics, and the like. These are to form the subject matter of a second volume.

The book begins with an introductory chapter on the aims and methods of education as the practising social psychologist sees them. It contains implicitly what the succeeding chapters are designed

Preface

to make explicit and usable. The main point is that without adequate motivation there can be no adequate learning, and that adequate motivation is a function not only of intellectual clarity and perception of goals, but of satisfactory social relations between pupils as much as between pupils and teachers.

To those who want to know what position this book takes as to the philosophies of education or theories about its ends, we would say, first, that we believe education to be concerned at least as much with laying the foundations for the development of society in the future as in the preservation of traditional skills and the traditional social structure. Secondly, we take this to imply in practice, that a child must grow not only in knowledge and skills, but also in democratic techniques of companionable co-operation in complex tasks and of bringing about social changes as the growth of technology and of other fields of knowledge demand them. The traditional textbooks for the teacher concentrate on the more conservative aspects of the acquisition of intellectual and other skills in classroom or laboratory. This book concentrates on the processes of social interaction, understanding and experience of which are vital in an era of the most rapid social and technical changes the world has ever seen.

Chapter 2 discusses in more detail the various roles of the teacher and the effects on classroom management of his position in the education hierarchy.

Chapter 3 is concerned with the important question of motivation. It thus follows on Chapter 1, and is also designed as an introduction to the more practical Chapters 4–9.

Chapters 4, 5, and 6 are quite specifically practical: how to use the sociometric method to create effective social groupings in the classroom; and what are the effects (and some of the difficulties) of such working in groups.

Since sociometric groupings should not be subjective or haphazard, Chapter 7 explains the use of objective test procedures. This in turn leads to the consideration of the 'problem' child and what to do about him (Chapter 8).

In Chapter 9, the question of examinations is taken up: what part do they play in the teaching and learning process, and how can they be made more effective?

Preface

The last chapter considers the problems arising just before the child leaves school, and discusses the teacher's approach to vocational guidance.

Throughout, there are link passages between the chapters, and cross-references.

An attempt has been made to keep the writing as free of specialist technical terminology as the subject matter allows. No attempt has been made to 'write down' or to produce a 'popular' handbook for amateurs. The book is meant for practising teachers or teachers in training; and it is hoped that they will not hesitate to send in criticisms and suggestions.

All authors had a hand in editing each others' chapters, but we should like particularly to thank Dr. E. R. Wyeth for the substantial help he gave when the volume as a whole was being prepared for the Press.

O. A. OESER

Department of Psychology
Melbourne University

September 1954

I

Society in Miniature:
The Social Roles of Pupil and Teacher
and their Relevance
to the Acquisition of Knowledge[1]

O. A. OESER

Synopsis

THIS chapter discusses the roles and social interactions of pupils and teachers in the classroom. It illustrates the findings of social psychology which are relevant to the problems of authority, of motivation to work and to learn, and of discipline. It leads into the following chapters by stating some fundamental principles of learning in a social setting which have implications for teaching practice, and ends by commenting on the desirability of giving the child continual opportunities for practising the principles and precepts of citizenship.

Introduction

The basic patterns of adult personality are built during infancy and childhood. Of crucial importance to the development of

---

[1] The substance of this chapter was delivered at the Teachers' College, University of Melbourne, as the John Smyth Memorial Lecture for 1950.

personalities, and therefore to the way in which a society functions, are the patterns of attitudes to authority.

During the development of the child three figures play the major—almost the exclusive—role in the formation of authority figures: the mother, the father, and the teacher. If these figures are experienced as benevolent, loving, security-giving and devoted to maintaining and increasing the child's conception of himself—his self-esteem or integrity—the child will grow up in good mental health, with an accepting yet independent attitude to society and its government. If the reverse is true—if early authorities are experienced as punishing, denying, frustrating—the child will grow up either with a submissive, passive set of attitudes, or as a rebellious and destructive citizen.

All children, during the years from five to fourteen, some much longer, spend the major part of the day in schools. Society compels them to do so and there expects them to be trained in its skills and mores so that, as adults, they can continually regenerate and enhance its structure and its potentialities. Consequently the nature of the miniature society in a school, and the quality and range of relationships between teachers and pupils as well as between pupils and pupils are of incalculable importance.

Education (in its most general sense) begins when a child is born and continues throughout life. In most pre-literate societies no formal instruction is given. In Western European societies formal instruction has been the rule since the times of classical Greece at least. The contents of instruction have changed markedly since the industrial revolution, but the processes have not changed to a comparable extent.

During the past fifty years, and especially in the past twenty, the development of general and social psychology has been having a profound influence both on concept and practice in education. It is that changing outlook which is reflected in the chapters of this book.

Briefly, it consists in paying far more attention to the nature and effects of group processes in the development of a balanced, mature personality.

The 'doctrine of formal discipline' maintained that specific kinds of learning had wider effects. Thus it was thought that learning poetry and prose by heart strengthened 'the memory' as a whole; or that learning a difficult subject like Latin or mathematics was a good discipline for strengthening 'the will'.

Experimental researches have shown, however, that this belief is false. Transfer of training from one field to another occurs only between closely related elements (5). Teachers know this very well from experience: pupils may do brilliant feats of memory in cricket scores or in history and fail to remember the elements of Latin or arithmetic, or even what home-work was set.

The question arises, 'Why does the child perform so unevenly?' According to the doctrine of formal discipline, his will ought to have been strengthened by having overcome difficulties in some studies. Failure then must be attributed to 'lack of concentration', 'laziness', or 'unwillingness'. Lack of interest, it is thought, should be overcome by the will.

Again, experimental researches have shown that learning and retention are poor when the learner is not interested, which is obvious enough, and that *interest is generated and sustained by social interactions more than by intellectual insight.*

The simplest way of illustrating this is by showing that there is a high correlation between a pupil's liking of a subject and his liking of the teacher (2). A second way is by demonstrating that the poor learners in a classroom are also poor in satisfactory relations with others in the class: the under-achievers are mostly found to be near isolates or even rejectees (see Chapters 5 and 6) and when their peer-relations are adjusted their learning also improves.

The matter can be put in a nutshell. *Children are affected by, and concerned with, the human qualities and the attitudes of the teacher to them as individuals, not with his technical competence, which is taken for granted.* Exactly the same is true of the relations between patients and nurses: patients judge nurses on their humanity, not on their technical efficiency. And just as the rate of convalescence is affected by the relations between nurse and patient, so the rate of learning is affected by the relations between teacher and pupil.

Some understanding of the many facets of social relations between teacher and pupils is therefore essential, if the practical advice given in later chapters is to be used to advantage.

O. A. Oeser

The social activities of teachers can be classified into two major sets of interrelationships:

> Relations between teachers and adults; and
> Relations between teachers and pupils.

These interrelations take place in various kinds of institutions: the schools, and the education departments or boards of governors. These, in turn, are part of the institutional framework of society as a whole.

By 'relations' is meant *the relations of a teacher in his professional capacity*. His relations with his colleagues or even with members of his family have sometimes to be taken into account when interpreting his behaviour in the classroom; but 'private' relations will here be disregarded and attention concentrated on 'public' relations.

The professional relations between a teacher and other adults fall into two classes: those between himself and the teaching hierarchy: colleagues, headmaster, inspector, director, minister of education; and those between himself and the parents of his pupils.

The former are discussed in Chapter 2 and the latter are touched upon in Chapter 6. Here it is necessary to make only two points. First, relations between teachers and between headmaster and staff are important to the pupils. No teacher faces his class as an isolated individual. He carries with him the attitudes he has formed elsewhere, and in his professional work, particularly, his professional attitudes and habits. Consequently, if he wishes an attitude of co-operativeness to carry conviction to his pupils, his attitude cannot be one of authoritarianism or of passive submissiveness in his relations with his own peers (3).

Secondly, his attitudes to parents should carry the same conviction. The most actively helpful attitude is one of quiet sympathetic listening, in an attempt to understand the conditions that are bearing on a child and on his family, before he undertakes to change matters through advice or counselling or giving orders. For instance, teachers often tell parents who inquire why a child has done badly, 'He does not pay attention; he won't concentrate'. Or they write in reports, 'if John *wanted* to, he could do better at arithmetic'. The real problems are, how has it come about that John does not want to and that the teacher and parents have not been able to get him to want; what are the forces which attract him elsewhere and push him away from arithmetic? Is it within the power of the teacher and the parents to alter the relative attractiveness of the goals? Will pressure or punishment in relation to his work in arithmetic make him like the subject or the teacher any better; and is it important for the learning process to like doing the subject? As soon as the teacher realizes that the blame for poor concentration lies not in the child's 'weakness of will', but that this weakness is the result of many complex social factors, then his power to alter the child's attitudes is very greatly increased. As in scientific work, only increased understanding brings about better control; impatience and coercion may succeed merely in distorting the apparatus. The simplest proof is again the repeated observation that there is a high correlation between liking a teacher and liking the subject he teaches. The simplest rule to remember is that no child, unless he is physically ill, is 'naturally' lazy.

The Teacher-Pupil roles

A mechanic has only one role in relation to his machines: to fit new parts and repair old ones. A teacher has many roles in relation to his pupils. Their range and the complexity of their interrelations make the teacher's task intrinsically one of the most interesting in the world and one of the most difficult, satisfying, and sometimes, nevertheless, frustrating.

Here is a list—by no means exhaustive—of the main roles he assumes when dealing with his pupils:

> instructor and clarifier, expert
> judge of achievements, assessor
> ethical preceptor, moralist
> legislator
> judge
> policeman
> friend and counsellor.

When he enters a class the teacher establishes a face-to-face relation with the class as a whole and with each individual child.

5

O. A. Oeser

The relation having been established, he begins to instruct in his subject. But it is soon clear that, although he is teaching the propositions and facts of subjects like history or geometry, he is also instructing the pupils in forms of behaviour: towards the task, towards himself, and towards other pupils. Right behaviour towards the task consists of completing it as given, to work hard, and to be neat and orderly. Right behaviour towards himself is to answer when questioned, to obey, to attend, be polite, be truthful. Right behaviour towards other pupils is to refrain from making distracting noises, cheating, chattering, bullying. He makes rules and polices them, and he makes judgments of all kinds in all kinds of matters from mathematics to morals. He acts as mediator and as adviser, clarifies difficulties, helps the clumsy, listens patiently and with friendly understanding to confidences about a child's anxieties or troubles at home. He rewards; and he punishes.

All the while he is also a representative of society, which has explicitly formulated his duties in laws and regulations; of the parents (since he is legally *in loco parentis*); and of adults or authority figures in general (Chapter 2).

As soon as one makes a survey of what it is that a teacher does, one realizes how small is the part actually played by the training in the skills of the three Rs. This was most vividly expressed by a Scottish headmaster, who many years ago, in a debate on the aims of education and the role of self-government in schools, said, 'education is the inculcation of a respect for authority'.

A more dispassionate way of looking at a teacher's activities is to investigate how pupils see the pressures that act on them in an ordinary classroom. As part of the Australian community and tensions studies of 1949–50, carried out on behalf of UNESCO, a detailed study was made of the school in a country town of Victoria (**2**, Chapters 10–12). Questions were asked of the pupils in the form, 'What is something you can do at school which is a good thing (a bad thing) to do?' and 'how are you praised (punished)?' The answers were classified into various 'activity areas':

(1) *Central:* activities directly connected with subject matter, e.g. 'studying hard' (good thing) or 'not doing home-work' (bad thing).

6

Society in Miniature

(2) *Peripheral:* activities connected with the incidental learning of ethical precepts and standards of behaviour (being fair to others, truthful, careful of school property).

(3) *Teacher Dominance:* activities which accept (as a good thing) or reject (as a bad thing) the dominance or authority of the teacher.

(4) *Child Restraint towards Teacher:* accepting or rejecting the specific restraints imposed by the teacher on his pupils (rules such as 'sit still', 'don't talk') or punishments in response to the child's acts of rebellion or aggression.

The following table (2, Table 101) shows the frequencies with which the teacher is mentioned as offering rewards or punishments in the classroom.

Activity Areas	Mentions of Teacher (percentages)			
	as Source of Reward		as Source of Punishment	
	Junior	Senior	Junior	Senior
	(N=73)	(N=166)	(N=177)	(N=164)
Central	12	7	2	5
Peripheral	48	54	1	14
Teacher Dominance	19	17	3	5
Child Restraint	21	22	94	76

This table shows very clearly that, in the eyes of the pupils, less than one-tenth of the rewarding or reproving behaviour of a teacher had to do with learning a subject.

The teacher, however, saw himself as being concerned with instructing: 'I cannot teach you arithmetic if you wriggle about and do not pay attention; if you distract Mary's attention she cannot learn'. True, he was also concerned that his pupils should develop behaviour which would be acceptable everywhere. But to him this was in one sense peripheral: standards of behaviour were important means through which the end of learning certain skills could be more efficiently achieved.

COMPLEMENTARY ROLES
COMPATIBLE AND INCOMPATIBLE DEFINITIONS OF BEHAVIOUR

The preceding shows that the classroom situation is, from the pupil's point of view especially, a social situation which is dominated by an authority figure. This finding is extremely important, because it enables the teacher to make use of quite different and much more powerful forces to control behaviour: the forces of interpersonal dynamics. Before we look at these more closely, however, one further conclusion must be drawn from the above table.

Suppose one asks a teacher, 'How should a pupil behave in class?' He will list a number of behaviours such as paying attention, concentrating on his work, writing neatly, being obedient, and so on. Having listed them, he can next rank them in order of importance. Let us suppose that for this particular teacher 'being obedient' ranks top, 'concentration' somewhere in the middle and 'being neat' at the bottom.

Suppose, next, that a pupil is asked the same question, and that he ranks the various behaviours in order of importance. If the same order is obtained, observation should show that this teacher and this pupil are in complete harmony: they see the situation in the same way and their value judgments agree. But suppose the rank orders are different and even that some quite different elements appear in the respective lists. Then we may expect clashes to occur, the reasons for which will be sought by the teacher in the pupil's 'personality': the pupil is thought to be 'lazy' or 'a liar'. The pupil in turn judges the teacher to be 'crabby', 'unreasonable' and generally to have the typical adult's incomprehension of the child's value systems.

Every role, then, has a complement: the set of rules which determines the actions of the teacher is balanced by a set of rules which determines the actions of the pupil. This works in four ways: (1) teachers expect pupils to behave in certain ways and (2) pupils expect teachers to behave in certain ways; (3) teachers define appropriate teacher behaviour and (4) pupils define pupil behaviour. The problem of morale and motivation in the classroom is solved when these four sets are complementary and not discrepant. When they are complementary, the necessity for punishment disappears; and when that happens, an enormous amount of energy is set free and can be devoted to more rewarding tasks.

The practical crux of the matter concerns the pupil's definitions of the expected and required behaviour of himself (and other pupils) towards the teacher and towards other pupils.

In a political democracy, rules of behaviour between authorities and citizens are arrived at through a long process of discussion, of trial and error, and by mutual agreement. Laws which are not accepted are not kept; group activities which cease to be regarded as rewarding to a group die out and, if they are sustained by threats of punishment, the interest is directed towards avoiding punishment and to leaving the situation as soon as possible.

This is undoubtedly one of the factors which is responsible for the great majority of children leaving school as soon as it is legally permissible. The only other factors are lack of mental ability to cope with academic work and the economic need of some families to increase their earnings. But observation and inquiry both show that pupils leave because they do not find the life of the classroom satisfying, they have not perceived and accepted the goals of formal education, and they therefore perceive the situation as one of coercion. This is another lesson to be drawn from the table on page 7.

One other fact needs to be emphasized. It is so well known that tables of figures are hardly necessary to illustrate it. This is that the subjects and activities at school which are best liked and which most frequently generate sustained attention are those in which considerable pupil interaction is possible: sports, crafts, and science. The subjects which are most strongly rejected are those in which the pupil is thrown on to his own resources and in which no amount of conscientious work can fully compensate for failing to meet the criteria of correctness: spelling and mathematics. In these he is most often subjected to the experience of repeated failure: both the teacher and the subject itself punish him (**2, 3**).

The Problem of Motivation

These considerations lead to the fundamental problems of motivation. Why is it that in a classroom motivation to learn can be so low that it has often to be artificially increased by punishment and other indirect incentives? Let us consider briefly what social psychology can contribute to this discussion, and what its implications are for classroom teaching.

Four important psychological propositions must be borne in mind. First, no behaviour is unmotivated in the psychological sense except reflex behaviour such as the knee-jerk or recovering lost balance. An organism is active when it is in a state of need. It then

9

O. A. Oeser

seeks a goal that will set this need at rest. Motivation is thus a name for the psycho-physiological processes that underlie goal-seeking activity. If a person is hungry and seeks food, he is motivated. If he is curious about the meaning of the sentence, 'Napoleon lost the Battle of Waterloo', and asks the history master or looks into a book, he is motivated to increase his knowledge, so as to set his curiosity at rest. If, on the other hand, a pupil is not curious, and is ordered to look it up, the teacher is using a spur or incentive, and the pupil will be motivated, not by the need to satisfy his curiosity, but by the need to escape punishment. That is why corporal punishment and marks are called 'indirect incentives', since the motivation they cause leads to learning only indirectly or incidentally.

The second proposition is that if a goal is too remote, or is not clearly enough perceived, activity ceases unless a substitute goal is found. A pupil aged twelve who is told that he must learn Latin because this will strengthen his intellect or his moral fibre or help him to get a better job, will learn Latin not through primary or intrinsic motivation but because a spur is applied by the teacher, so giving rise to a secondary or extrinsic motivation. In addition, he is quite likely to learn to dislike Latin or even all formal learning.

This leads to a third proposition: that no item of knowledge becomes part of a person's total pattern of knowledge unless there is emotional acceptance as well as cognitive understanding. This can be clearly seen in the fact that even an intelligent pupil will often do badly in a subject he dislikes.

The last observation leads to the fourth proposition: that two of the most powerful and persistent human needs are the need for social acceptance and the need for communication. If a teacher is disliked, or if he dislikes a pupil, there are barriers to both acceptance and communication.

The importance of adequate communication is shown by the fact that the process of psychotherapy depends on the ability of the psychologist to help the patient to overcome barriers because of which the patient cannot communicate the real nature of his anxieties. The importance of social acceptance can be understood from the fact that the problem child in a class is also an isolate, that is, he is not accepted by his classmates and is excluded from their cliques or teams (see Chapter 7).

Society in Miniature

This analysis began by saying that the basic problem of all teaching is to arouse adequate motivation that directs activity to appropriate goals. The other propositions—that goals must not be too remote, that adequate learning depends on emotional acceptance as well as on understanding, and that social acceptance and ease of communication are persistent needs—are closely related to the first. Unless there is adequate motivation, all incentives tend to deflect learning—*all* learning; the learning of social and ethical habits as well as the learning of intellectual skills—from its proper goals.

Another way of looking at these psychological propositions is as follows: for action to occur, there must be a goal which must be perceived *and accepted* for motivation to be generated. Further, in social action (of which learning and teaching are examples) a person must feel himself to be an accepted member of a group. This is a complex way of saying that a pupil 'must want' to co-operate with the teacher, and also with the class as a whole, the group goals of which he accepts. Conversely, the goals of teacher and pupils must be defined in the same terms. To be active intellectually, physically, and socially is the most characteristic feature of childhood. What a school should do is to create an environment in which the child can be active in all these ways, not one in which he is merely the passive recipient of instruction. The child should be the worker; and the teacher's job is to create a permissive environment in which clarification and instruction serve to fulfil the needs of pupils.

The Dilemmas of Education

Consider the standard classroom. In general, pupils are not permitted to communicate with each other freely; they are forced into competition with each other; teachers believe in the 'doctrine of formal discipline'; and teachers are obliged to use incentives or spurs, among which corporal and verbal punishments take a high place. Lastly, consider that schools and society are disconnected, so much so that parents rarely visit them except on formal occasions; and that as regards the practices of political democracy schools and society are considerably at variance.

The Way Out

The way out of these dilemmas is now clear. It consists simply in breaking up the class into small groups and allowing them full freedom of speech with these sole restrictions: that the discussions within the group must be relevant to the topic being studied and that the level of noise must not be such as to prevent other groups from working. The second restriction soon becomes unnecessary, since the groups themselves will see to it that others do not unduly disturb them (Chapter 6).

Though the method is easy to grasp, it is not simple to apply. The class should not be split into groups haphazardly. The method which should be used is a combination of sociometry and psychometrics. Detailed discussions of these will be found in Chapters 4 to 6. Briefly, sociometry studies the kind and intensity of social relations between pupils, and psychometrics assesses the intellectual capacity and attainments of the individual. Combining these two methods enables the teacher to make groupings that are emotionally satisfying and efficient for the tasks in hand. Put very simply, the processes which work so well in games and in the workshop or laboratory are applied to all formal subjects.

What teachers who do this will find is that the output of work will be multiplied many times and that learning will be not only speeded up but will be better retained and, above all, better liked. The amount of knowledge gained by a pupil is of little importance in future life if the road to it has been emotionally frustrating. If it has, he will not use it in his leisure, though he may be forced to use it in earning a living.

The most remarkable result of the sociometric grouping of pupils is not so much that they work harder, learn more and retain better, but that the tensions between pupils are diminished below those thought to be normal in ordinary play. This is because the barriers to social acceptance and to communication are removed. The direct consequence of this is that most of the tensions between pupils and teacher vanish. Any teacher who is well integrated and secure can thus attain affection and respect freely given. There is nothing mysterious in this. Tact, and the ability to deal easily with children, used to be thought a personality characteristic. It can, however, be learned because we now understand more clearly the dynamics of social fields and the forces at play in the interaction of individuals.

Society in Miniature

'CLARIFICATION' AND 'TACT'

One other step has to be taken. The teacher must strip himself of his status consciousness and be willing to be accepted because of his superior knowledge and skills, not because of his greater physical strength and the power behind his institutional status. In other words, the teacher must become a leader in knowledge and wisdom, not an officer who must be obeyed. To achieve this is not as hard as it may sound. All teachers are fond of their pupils and take pride in their work. That love is the greatest constructive force in the world has been understood ever since organisms attained self-consciousness. What the social sciences have done is to give man better insight into practical ways of expressing his affection and using it for constructive ends. A brief case history will illustrate this assertion.

A Scottish working-class mother asked for advice about her daughter, aged ten, who was refusing food, was dropping behind at school, was pale and listless. The doctor could find nothing wrong and advised a more stimulating diet plus cod liver oil, and urged the mother to see to it that the child ate more. Both doctor and parents failed, and the situation was getting serious. The mother was interviewed by the psychologist who by explaining in simple terms the psychology of fear and withdrawal reactions persuaded her to say to the child when she again refused her evening meal: 'Never mind, Jean, I'll keep it for you, you may feel hungry later.' The child also refused to go to sleep and would lie awake for many hours. He said, 'When she says "I won't go to sleep," say to her: "Never mind, if you're nice and warm in bed, you'll be getting all the rest you need."'

She reported two days later. The child had looked astonished, and had said nothing, but had asked for her tea an hour later. When put to bed with the new formula, she was asleep in half an hour.

The point of this story is that these parents loved their child. But their traditional role as Scottish parents required authority on their part and obedience on the part of the children. Like teaching, medicine has become mechanized and split into fractions. That doctor's notion was that if food could be got into the stomach, physiological processes would do the rest. How to get the food into the stomach was the parents' job. The child felt that since the arrival of a younger

13

O. A. Oeser

sister she was no longer the centre of the little social group; she felt socially unaccepted. But, being a child, she could not communicate this to her parents in ways which they would understand. The psychologist perceived these role relationships and needs, and was able to direct the love of the parents to other means of achieving their goal—the well-being of the child.

The child was a problem for her teacher too. She was too preoccupied with her own emotional difficulties to be able to concentrate on her work—and in some schools concentration is regarded as a positive virtue; lack of concentration as a vice to be punished. So she got into trouble with the class teacher and also with the other children, who teased her because she would not play in the normal way. She was physically listless from lack of food and sleep. But more important was that her fantasy of being rejected by her intimate social group began to be a feeling of being rejected by all social groups. To her mind, the teacher's growing pressure was, of course, a proof of this.

The other part of the therapeutic process consisted, therefore, in explaining to the teacher what the psychological situation was, and getting his co-operation. Like many teachers, he had never considered lack of concentration as resulting from anything other than lack of desire to apply will-power. But he genuinely liked children, and so little Jean's therapy was dramatically rapid at school also.

This case history shows that the goal desired by parents, doctor, and teacher was the same, namely, improvement in the mental and physical health of the child. Only the means were wrong. If there had been adequate communication between these three, and if they had been aware of the nature and consequences of social forces, they could have found the solution of the child's difficulties themselves. But neither the teacher nor the doctor communicated with, or investigated, the family as a social group.

For similar reasons, the means used by teachers to achieve their goal—the development of citizens actively interested in social process and flexible enough to continue to learn—require changing. And the modern developments in the social sciences have given us enough insight to be able to do so reasonably well (1).

Education is an applied social science. Fifty years ago there was no social science worthy of the name. Even thirty years ago psychology itself (except for the work of Sigmund Freud) was preoccupied with

14

problems of perception, learning, volition, attention, thought, memory, and imagination, all conceived of as processes within the individual that had nothing to do with the individual as a focus of social forces. Emotion was outside the psychologist's scope. It was thought to have something to do with instincts and to be able perhaps to affect the imagination, but was otherwise not worthy of intellectual attention.

During the past generation this situation has changed radically. The brief case history illustrates how knowledge and the insight into complex relations which it gives can give to human aspirations greater power for achieving their aims. In medicine or engineering this is, of course, obvious. But it also shows that mental health is a concept that includes physical health and with it the whole social, intellectual, and emotional development of a child.

Conclusion

Many of the traditional methods used in the classroom are faulty because they rest on inadequate insight into social structure and function; because they rest on an out-of-date psychology; because they are inefficient to the point of wastefulness; and because they too often induce anxiety and a desire to escape from knowledge. That a curriculum can be sliced into small portions, that there are steps up the ladder to the goal of knowledge and that if the pupil cannot see the goal clearly he ultimately will if he can be made to take the steps, are implicit assumptions which are demonstrably false. Each goal, however near, must be clearly perceived, understood, and accepted by the individual pupil and by his peer groups. The process of perceiving and clarification needs discussion and mutual support; it is not attained merely because the teacher exercises pressure. Punishment does not drive a pupil to the goal desired by education, it deflects him to quite different goals.

In our society there is a gulf between political and educational practice (4). We believe in, and largely practise, political democracy. That is, as citizens we elect our representatives and thus our governments, whether local or national. If we do not approve of its actions or goals, we elect another. Bertrand Russell has remarked that from history we should by now have learnt one truth: the reason for democracy is that it is impossible in practice to find a collection of

O. A. Oeser

men, however wise, to whom government can safely be entrusted in perpetuity. If the practice of democracy is not taught by precept and training in our schools, it can hardly be assumed with safety that our institutions are built on firm foundations.

SELECTED REFERENCES FOR FURTHER READING

1. CURRY, W. B., *The School* (London, John Lane, 1934). This book, by the headmaster of one of the most interesting 'progressive' or 'experimental' schools in England, is well worth reading in conjunction with Chapters 1–3. It considers the kinds of attitudes which are required if education is to keep pace with the rapidly changing social structure of the world. In particular, the chapters on 'Freedom and Discipline', 'Competition and Marks', 'Co-education' and 'The Intellectual Climate' are brilliant essays in the theory and practice of modern education.

2. OESER, O. A., and EMERY, F. E., *Social Structure and Personality in a Rural Community* (London, Routledge & Kegan Paul, 1954). Chapter 10 deals with the ways in which a school brings about integration within a community through the pupils. Chapter 11 shows in what ways the school integrates the community with society at large. Chapter 12 is a detailed study of the school in action and of the ways in which pupils perceive and experience their relations to the teacher and to the subject matter he teaches.

3. OESER, O. A., and HAMMOND, S. B. (eds.) *Social Structure and Personality in a City* (London, Routledge & Kegan Paul, 1954). Part IV is concerned with the ways in which children develop age and sex roles. Chapter 15 analyses the relation between the social climate in the family and the child's adjustment at school, and Chapter 16 deals with the pressures exerted by the school and the child's reaction.

4. OTTAWAY, A. K. C., *Education and Society. An Introduction to the Sociology of Education* (London, Routledge & Kegan Paul, 1953). In a brief compass, this book gives an introduction to the relations between school and the various forces of society. It discusses the kinds of social forces which bring about cultural change, the social determinants of education in England, and the kinds of educational needs which our changing society is developing. Chapter 7, 'The School as a Social Unit', discusses pupil participation and self-government, and the social climate of the school.

5. WEBB, L. W., 'Transfer of Learning', pp. 522–548 of Skinner, Charles E. (ed.), *Educational Psychology* (London, Staples Press, 3rd edn., 1952; New York, Prentice-Hall). This chapter gives a not too technical exposition of the doctrine of formal discipline, of the experimental work which has tested it, and of the conclusions to be drawn from work on transfer of training.

16

II

The Teacher in the Educational Hierarchy

and the Teacher and the

Curriculum

E. R. WYETH and W. C. WATSON

Synopsis

Two questions are asked whenever teachers discuss the development of a permissive or 'democratic' social climate in schools: How can this be done when the headmaster, fixed in traditional methods, insists upon a well-disciplined school? (The headmaster may ask a similar question when his staff or the inspectors are conservative.)

How can I establish child-centred methods when I have a prescribed curriculum to follow?

This chapter discusses certain implications of these two questions. It does not attempt to give direct answers for the obvious reason that to neither question is a direct answer possible. In some circumstances the answers would have to be that it would be impossible to establish a democratic social climate. In others, closer examination of the situation and understanding of the influences operating might show ways of overcoming the difficulties.

17

E. R. Wyeth and W. C. Watson

The first question carries deeper implications than the winning of the headmaster's permission to embark upon the new methods. The very fact of its being asked suggests that the teacher is aware of his subordinate place in a professional or administrative hierarchy and of limitations which this imposes upon his behaviour. These limitations are obvious because they are, to some extent at least, part of the accepted structure of school organization. They are not the only factors which modify or determine a teacher's activities in the school. Instead of answering the question asked, an attempt will be made to examine some of these determining factors in the hope that a greater understanding of their significance may help the teacher to overcome the difficulties they cause.

Most writers on educational method lay some stress upon the teacher's personality as an essential for successful teaching. The pupils will react to the teacher's manner, his way of doing things, his behaviour. But to be told that one must develop a 'pleasing manner', a 'stimulating personality', or a 'sympathetic attitude' is not much help. Teachers need to understand what makes them behave as they do in the various situations with which they are faced. Francis J. Brown (1) gives a useful definition of personality:

'Human nature is socially acquired. The individual becomes a person only through social interaction. These two statements form the basis of our definition of personality: *personality is the person's concept of his role in social groups*. This concept determines his behaviour within the group.

'Personality, however, is not fixed and static, but is constantly changing in terms of the roles, assumed or actual, which the person ascribes to himself in relation to his *environments*. The plural is used deliberately because the person's status varies in different situations. From these many concepts of status, the person accrues a more stable sense of his own role so that his behaviour in a given situation can be predicted with some assurance.'

This concept of the personality of the individual, of the teacher, emphasizes the importance of his own concept of the role he is playing. His concepts of himself, and of his activities, will largely determine his attitudes and behaviour towards his pupils (and theirs

18

towards him) and will therefore be a major factor in determining the social climate of the classroom.

In the complex social situation which the average classroom presents with the constant interplay of thirty or more personalities, the teacher fills many roles—the instructor dispensing knowledge, the assessor estimating standards of achievement, the moralist giving judgments upon right and wrong, the judge determining guilt, the policeman maintaining school 'law' and inflicting punishment, and the legislator making new 'laws', to give names to but a few. These, and the many like them, are the transitory roles which every teacher plays so often that he no longer notices the changes in his behaviour which they involve. It might be a salutary experience for the teacher to observe these chameleon-like changes in his behaviour during a normal school day.

Behind these transitory roles may be identified others which are more general and more significant to the teacher who attempts to clarify his responsibility as leader of a democratic school group:

1. He is a member of the teaching hierarchy in the general educational system and in the school.

2. He is a representative of a particular subculture of society.

3. He is the subject matter expert, the acknowledged superior of his class in this specialized knowledge.

4. He is the methodologist, the expert in procedures for study and learning.

5. He is a counsellor, assessing, advising, and arranging situations to overcome tensions and facilitate development.

6. He is a representative of adult society, to whom the children will react in different ways, as they do to other adults.

These roles warrant consideration in more detail:

The Teacher as a Member of the Teaching Hierarchy

In view of the question posed in the introduction, this role of the individual teacher, be he assistant or principal, requires close examination.

School organization, in most countries, usually results in a status hierarchy among the teachers. Within a school the formal organization gives the principal the highest status, and then, through steps of seniority, downwards to the student. With formal status goes a varying measure of responsibility. The principal is responsible to the educational authority, represented by the inspector, for the complete management of his school. The individual teacher is responsible to the principal, sometimes through a senior teacher, for the management of that part of the school's operation allotted to him.

Behind the formal hierarchy lie the less tangible but functionally more important personal relationships which may or may not conform to the formal pattern, and which may or may not be strictly hierarchical. In the strictly hierarchical structure the general relationship is likely to be authoritarian, the principal imposing his management of the school upon the staff. The teacher, who sees his professional role as part of such a hierarchy, and who accepts that role, is in a frame of mind which makes it impossible for him to create a co-operative atmosphere in the classroom.

A closer examination of the non-formal relationships among the staff of a school does show potentialities for the successful establishment of a co-operative atmosphere, the principal acting as leader to promote those conditions under which intelligent discussion flourishes and the energies of the staff and students are released; the teacher conceiving himself as a member of a group working towards an objective decided upon by the group.

The formal structure is by no means rigid. While the principal must accept responsibility for the working of his school, it is now common for most principals to leave most of the procedure of class management to the individual teachers so long as they are satisfied that certain general requirements are met. While seniority is the chief factor determining the position of a teacher in the formal hierarchy, it does not alone determine a teacher's prestige. The teacher's academic background, the variety of his experiences, his capacity as a teacher (formally rated by an inspector) all tend to give him a prestige independent of his place in the formal hierarchy. Mobility within the hierarchy also reduces its rigidity. It is normally expected that a teacher will progress upwards in classification. In the State primary schools of Victoria, for instance, there is little status value within the profession attached to the terms 'head teacher' and 'assistant', for the individual may occupy either position, transferring voluntarily from one to the other within the same classification. This, however, must not be regarded as typical of all Australian states.

The Teacher in the Educational Hierarchy

In some the head teacher, especially in larger schools, enjoys a much higher status than his assistants.

This brief consideration of some of the factors at present reducing the rigidity of the hierarchical structure of a school staff is given to indicate that there is the possibility of an effective co-operative organization within the present formal structure. There is, in fact, nothing in the formal organizational requirements themselves which prevents the staff from working together as a co-operative organization. The staff meeting can be a worth-while group experience. It will need to delineate clearly the goals it is setting out to attain and to work objectively to achieve a group decision upon action, towards which each individual has made some positive contribution and with which he feels himself positively identified. This sort of group does not just happen; it can be created only gradually by individuals aware of the dynamics of social interaction and ready to make objective assessments of their own group behaviour. A co-operative social climate among the school staff would be the best guarantee of a similar climate in the classroom.

If this fully co-operative staff organization cannot be achieved, the teacher's responsibility for his own class makes imperative an attempt to generate the desired social climate there. It is needless to point out the greater difficulty of organizing small units on this basis in the midst of a general authoritarian environment. Before attempting such a limited change, the teacher concerned should make a careful estimate of the strength of the authoritarian 'climate' in which his class will be working. The tensions developed in his pupils by the dual environment might endanger the project and harm the children.

A second assessment which he must make is of the role in which he sees himself while undertaking the project. Perhaps the greatest danger of working alone upon the project is that the teacher will so identify the maintenance or enhancement of his own professional prestige with the 'success' of his project that, from the children's point of view, he is merely imposing a different procedure upon them. By seeing himself as a unit in a competitive professional group he makes it unlikely that the class will see him as a co-operative partner in the experiences. The teacher then must face the question, 'Is my relationship with the staff of the school such that I can work as a dispassionate, objective leader with the children?'

E. R. Wyeth and W. C. Watson

The Teacher as a Representative of a Particular Subculture of Society

As a member of a subculture of society—a lower middle-class, Protestant, urban society perhaps—the teacher will have acquired certain political biases, philosophical leanings, cultural goals, and perceptions of social customs. These will influence his classroom relationships as he expresses his opinion, interprets social events of the past or present, and generally contributes to the group feelings and attitudes. His membership of his particular subculture has brought with it certain kinds of social interaction through which his personality has developed. Unless he recognizes that the social interactions of his pupils outside the school may be in a different subculture, the teacher stands in danger of seriously misinterpreting their behaviour and of expecting motivation towards goals which, though significant to him, are interpreted differently by the children.

The teacher must thus become a social analyst. Not only must he analyse his own subculture objectively, but he must examine carefully his own biases, attitudes and customs. His analysis must include the leanings and customs of his students and in interpreting these— and his own—he has an important responsibility.

The Teacher as a Representative of Adult Society

All the problems of subculture differences are increased by the fact that, to the pupils, the teacher is a representative of adult society. From this point of view the teacher has a complex role. Some children may view him as a symbol of authority—the adult authority— against which they have been virtually defenceless all their lives; others may see him as a representative of the opposite sex. Some may establish a child-father or child-mother relationship and bring to the classroom the problems they have in their relationship with their own parents.

The fact that the pupils expect the teacher to behave as an adult leaves him no option but to accept the role. In playing it, however, his reactions may have important effects upon the pupils.

The chief requirements of the situation are to perceive the real needs of each pupil in establishing a particular type of relationship and to accept objectively all the responsibilities of guidance that may be involved.

The Teacher in the Educational Hierarchy

He must be aware of the dynamics of child society and, by encouraging freer group activities, prevent the activities of children's groups from being directed against adult society and himself.

With students of secondary school age there is an added danger. They are already moving into adult society themselves and are learning that its reality does not always conform to what they as children were led to believe. It is not uncommon for adolescents to perceive the teacher as the representative of this child-conceived adult society and as a species apart from real adults.

The Teacher as a Counsellor

The diverse needs of the group call for great skill from the teacher as a personal and educational counsellor. The problems of group participation require careful handling in order that the energies of the members may be released and employed to best advantage. As a member of the group his relationships with other members vary greatly and may call for extremely skilful handling.

It is as a counsellor rather than as a policeman that the teacher should approach the problem of maintaining discipline. This does not mean that police action may not sometimes be necessary. It does mean that, wherever a problem arises, it should be noted as a symptom of group disturbance and, whatever immediate action might be taken, diagnosis and correction of the real cause of the tensions and disturbance are still necessary.

The standard by which behaviour is judged should arise from implicit or explicit group decisions and should be maintained by the group of which the teacher is an accepted member. (This aspect is more fully developed in Chapters 4–6.)

The Teacher as a Subject-Matter Expert and Methodologist

These two roles are, of course, especially characteristics of the teacher within the classroom group, and co-operative organization will make greater demands upon his skill than authoritarian teaching. It is a misunderstanding of learning and teaching which has led some teachers who use child-centred and activity programmes to withhold their knowledge from the children in the expectation that the children should find out for themselves. The psychological basis for

E. R. Wyeth and W. C. Watson

group methods is the strong motivation to learning engendered within a co-operative group. But the children can perceive the problem only in relation to their own past experience and present needs. Only the teacher can see the possible learning which can take place in the impending experiences, and only he can see beforehand the lines of development, the facts to be known, and the skills to be acquired in order that the pupils should attain their goals expeditiously and with a minimum of failure and frustration.

The rapidity with which children can assimilate information under strong motivation has surprised teachers who have been used to the slow and often tedious development of a concept by the class teaching method. Class teachers know that simply to tell the class some fact is usually ineffective unless it is fortified by pictorial and other aids, repetition, exercises, and even drill. But if the group is aware of its immediate need for the information, the simple telling of the fact is often all that is necessary. Group learning can be so rapid and extensive that the teacher needs far more subject matter readily available than he would require for a class lesson. There will be ample opportunity for the children to find things out for themselves in those situations which require actual experience as an essential for understanding. The concept of the values of weights can be gained only by handling weights and weighing things. A teacher's statement that there are 16 oz. in 1 lb. cannot create the concept though it may become explicit if it follows experience.

The teacher's usual role as a methodologist must undergo re-orientation if co-operative group work is to be successful. Under class teaching the techniques and methods he tends to develop are those by which *he* can best present the subject matter to the pupils. Under group methods he must place his emphasis upon the methods and techniques to be employed by *the children* to ensure the satisfactory development of their activities and learning.

PART II. THE CURRICULUM

The second question, how child-centred methods can be established when a prescribed curriculum has to be followed, is asked by most teachers who are considering any change in their classroom organization or teaching method. It is true that the prescribed curriculum does set limits upon the teacher, and the more rigidly prescribed the course, the greater the limitations.

It is usually the case in Australian States that in the primary school curriculum and in the secondary syllabus below matriculation, the courses set out are, to some extent, in broad outline only, and the teacher is free, under certain conditions, to adapt the prescribed content of subjects taught. It is not sufficient for him simply to vary the subject matter presented to the children, although there might be some advantage in meeting specially strong interests by such changes where possible.

More important is the teacher's view of the purpose of the prescribed course. Perhaps the most common view is that the course sets out the list of skills and aspects of knowledge which the pupils are to acquire. From such a viewpoint methods, techniques, and organization are considered only for their effectiveness in facilitating the instructions. The best methods will be those which enable the children to acquire the skills or information most readily and to retain them. Success is measured by an examination of the amount of knowledge retained or of the quality of the skilled performance.

The wider view of child development presented by this volume requires a different view of the curriculum. This is already suggested in the Victorian 'General Course of Study for Primary Schools, 1934'. An excerpt follows:

'It is vital that in his (the teacher's) interpretation (of the curriculum) the emphasis should be transferred from the subject to the growing child, and that the teaching of each subject should be looked upon not as an end itself, but as a means towards the complete development of the pupils. Finally, the pupil will fully develop in the best sense only through participation in purposeful activities with his fellows.' (p. 455).

The curriculum must be looked upon as part of the content of a set of experiences, planned not merely to facilitate knowledge of this content but to meet the child's continually developing and expanding needs.

The essential features of a course of study organized in experience units are set out by W. H. Burton (2) and compared with subject-matter units:

25

E. R. Wyeth and W. C. Watson

SUBJECT-MATTER UNITS	EXPERIENCE UNITS:
... begin, in the intention of adults, to teach approved subject matter to pupils;	... begin, in the intention of the learner, to achieve some purpose; to satisfy some need;
... are organized logically around a core within the subject matter;	... are organized psychologically around a purpose of the learner;
... are prepared in advance, by a person or group already familiar with materials and their logic;	... are organized as they develop by a group facing a new situation for the first time;
... are for the purpose of having the pupil acquire the logically arranged subject matter;	... are for the immediate purpose of satisfying needs of the learner and with the ultimate purpose of developing desirable understandings, attitudes, skills, etc., in the learner
... are usually organized from simple to complex and within subject fields;	... are usually organized functionally and in disregard of subject lines, especially in elementary grades; often from complex to simple; (the complex urbanized, industrialized civilization within which a child lives is often more comprehensible than the simple life of primitive peoples. Child has no experience with the latter, much with the former);
... are controlled by the teacher, by adult committee, by course of study;	... are controlled by a co-operating group of learners which includes the teacher; the course of study is utilized as needed;
... are usually centred in the past, in the 'accumulated, not the accumulating' culture; little reference to present or future; reference to future usually theoretical;	... are usually centred in present and future; use accumulated materials from past freely in solving present problems;
... rely on formal methods, assignments, distinct lesson types, printed materials as chief sources, learning experiences few and formal;	... utilize co-operatively planned procedures suited to situation, sources in great variety, learning experiences numerous and varied;

The Teacher in the Educational Hierarchy

SUBJECT-MATTER UNITS	EXPERIENCE UNITS:
... give all pupils the same contact with the same materials; some provision for individual differences;	... give contacts with many materials; individual differences cared for variously and automatically;
... have fixed outcomes which are known in advance and are required uniformly for all learners;	... do not have fixed outcomes which are known in advance, and required uniformly from all learners;
... at conclusion, evaluate through the use of formal tests of subject-matter acquisition, usually of fact or skill;	... evaluate many complex outcomes, continuously, with constant pupil participation and through use of many instruments, formal and informal;
... close with a backward look, so-called 'review', and are done with when finished.	... lead to new interests, problems, and purposes.

The organization of the curriculum into experience units is presented here to illustrate the view of the curriculum necessary for a democratic 'climate' in the classroom and not as a single method by which the many skills and items of knowledge will emerge automatically. If the co-operative spirit has been established and its dynamics fully understood by the teacher, any method may be regularly used. The class-lesson may still be most suitable for some topics—but the children will be actively following their teacher in satisfying what is recognized as a common need and not as passive receivers of information prepared and presented by the teacher for reasons which he alone knows. The children may work individually or in pairs upon drills and exercises, each individual progressing at a rate determined by his own ability. If the children have a clear understanding of the goal and are motivated towards its attainment. that method is best which leads them to the goal most quickly. It is tedious and irritating for a child to have to search out information which he knows the teacher could tell him in a few minutes.

One problem faced by the teacher who attempts to use the children's immediate interests as motivation for their learning is to lead the children's development towards adult living. It cannot be assumed that the experiences of the ordinary day-to-day work in the

27

classroom will of themselves lead to such development. It is the teacher's responsibility to use the children's present interests and concepts for arousing their awareness of new and advanced goals. The prescribed curriculum is usually planned with such a development in mind and, in following this, the teacher must ensure that the class is aware of the ultimate objectives and appreciates the immediate goals as significant for their own needs. He must, of course, do this without being autocratic or treating these goals as though they were another part of the curriculum which has to be *learned* in the same way.

Where curricula are prescribed in broad outline and not in detail, a considerable measure of local adaptation is possible. Much planning falls upon the headmaster and staff. Overall planning must be done at general staff meetings. Details must then be considered by the teacher or teachers of each subject and each teacher should have a clear picture of desirable goals and methods. The next stage of planning is set in the classroom where teacher and pupils together decide upon objectives and consider methods of reaching them. Further planning of individual activities may then be the function of small groups within the classroom.

At the completion of each unit and at the end of each course evaluation must take place—not necessarily by teacher-prepared examination—and it must be in terms of the objectives decided upon at the beginning of the course. In other words, this evaluation must be in terms readily understood by the pupils and appreciated by them as being an objective statement of the degree to which they have attained their goals rather than as a personal assessment of abilities in such a way as to imply praise and blame. The teacher's objective attitude must be evident in his method of evaluation and the evaluation process must be seen by the pupils as a step towards their goal, not as the goal itself. (This is more fully developed in Chapter 9.)

The sequence of development of a course of study would proceed in the following general cycle:

(*a*) to assess the state of affairs and diagnose the needs within the group;

(*b*) to plan activities, based upon a prescribed course if required, to meet these needs;

(*c*) to carry through the activities planned;
(*d*) to evaluate the success of the activities;
(*e*) to reassess;
(*f*) to replan, and so on in successive cycles.

SELECTED REFERENCES FOR FURTHER READING

1. BROWN, FRANCIS J., *Educational Sociology.* London, The Technical Press Ltd., 1947).
2. *National Society for the Study of Education, Forty-ninth Yearbook, Learning and Instruction* (University of Chicago Press, 1950). A very useful reference book for teachers. Few books, if any, surpass it as a teacher's handbook.
3. BRADFORD, BENNE, LIPPITT, *et al.* Articles on group dynamics in education. *N.E.A. Journal.* 1948, Vol. 37, Nos. 6, 7, 8. These articles are not very technical and are of much interest to teachers.
4. SNYGG, DONALD and COMBS. ARTHUR W., *Individual Behaviour* (New York, Harper, 1949).

III

The Social Conditions for
Successful Learning

H. A. PRESSER, G. W. D. BOYD, and R. C. G. LEA

Synopsis

CHAPTER 1 has discussed in general terms the major problems of education and some of the relations between school and society. It stressed the need for arousing adequate, goal-directed motivation as the essential condition for effective learning to take place.

Since the problem of the nature and phases of motivation is so important, this chapter expands the argument. It aims to give the teacher a more thorough grasp of this topic, before he attempts to appreciate and, later, to apply to classroom practice the methods of social psychology.

Preface

Although the book as a whole is not intended to be a theoretical exposition of the psychological problems of teaching, this chapter is fairly heavily weighted with theory. It has been included because an understanding of the principles discussed in it is of crucial importance for the practising teacher. It has an unusually large list of references for further reading, intended for those who wish to make a very thorough study of the subject.

The Social Conditions for Successful Learning

The best plan for the student is to read this chapter through fairly quickly, then read Chapters 4 to 6, and then re-read this Chapter carefully, following up with some of the suggested references.

Introduction

How important is 12.15? The ringing of the school bell at 12.15 means much the same thing to teachers as to children. Both are hungry—they need food; both are fatigued—they need relaxation. In a history lesson, 12.15 signifies the signing of Magna Carta. Do the teacher and children see 12.15 here from the same point of view? The goals of teacher and children are the same at lunch hour on any school day. Are they the same during a history lesson?

All behaviour is initiated by some need. In school A the children under the influence of a pressing need to satisfy their curiosity which has been aroused by an interesting and stimulating discussion, disregard the school bell. Teachers and children continue their researches until this particular need diminishes, or until the need for food can no longer be ignored. In school A the goals of teacher and children appear to be indistinguishable.

To the children in school B the school bell at 12.15 may represent a welcome escape from the teacher's formal cross-examination about this period of history.

Many teachers are familiar with the tremendous release of physical energy occasioned by the ringing of the school bell, the visible relaxation of the class, the outbreak of excited chatter, the feverish groping for the lunch bag, the rush on to the playground.

Motivation. The differences between the behaviour of the children in schools A and B arise from differences between the needs that have been initiated in the respective classrooms. The children are said to be differently 'motivated'. By motivation is meant an internal process, which is initiated by a need, and which leads to goal-seeking activity. The goal-seeking activity is aimed at satisfying that need.

Incentives. 'Motivations' must be clearly distinguished from 'incentives'. An incentive is some object or process other than the need developed during study of a subject, which determines the nature and direction of activity. If a child 'wants' to learn more about Magna Carta because he is interested, because his previous studies have left him with the promise of further exciting reading or discovery or

31

because he wants the answer to some questions which have occurred to him, he is motivated. If he 'wants' to learn because he wishes to please his parents or teacher, or show off to his fellows, or gain marks, punishment, praise, rivalry, and reward are said to be incentives.

Put in a different way: incentives are analogous to spurs and are administered by external causes; motivations arise within the person when a need has been created, such as a problem which insistently calls for a solution, or the excitement of discovery. If a pupil says, 'I *want* to know more because I am interested', he is motivated; if the teacher says 'You *must want* to know more', it is the teacher who is applying an incentive, because he has the power to insist.

How Needs Arise

Physical needs arise for the maintenance of life and for normal development of the organism.

In the classroom this means: A child, who feels cold, hungry, thirsty, or who needs to visit the toilet, cannot be expected to work effectively.

All Behaviour is Directed Towards Need Satisfaction

A young animal is born with the ability to move freely and to satisfy most of its needs by its own efforts, but the human infant is dependent on a social group—the family—for the satisfaction of its basic physical needs.

A very young infant in need of food begins to cry and continues to do so until the necessary food is provided. When an infant becomes aware that objects necessary to satisfy his physical needs exist in an external environment, much of his behaviour is directed at attempting to control that environment. From this stage of development, he acquires *social needs* which stem from his attempts at gaining satisfaction for his physical needs through others. When his needs are frustrated, he experiences feelings of anxiety and insecurity and these painful states urgently demand relief.

He learns that certain types of behaviour lead to need satisfaction, and that social acceptance of his behaviour alleviates his anxiety and makes him feel more secure as a member of a group. Certain other forms of behaviour do not lead to need satisfaction, and his feelings

32

of anxiety and insecurity may be intensified. This point may be illustrated by a simple example:

By getting a sum right a child experiences the satisfaction of having completed a task, and in addition may receive recognition by his teacher and his classmates. As a result the child will feel competent and secure. He will attempt more and even difficult sums of the same type.

But the child who has made a genuine effort to get a sum right and has not been successful may not only feel keen personal disappointment, but in addition may be rebuked by his teacher. The effect of this may well be that he will feel even more incompetent and insecure, and will in future be less willing to attempt sums of the same or even lesser difficulty.

Need Satisfaction occurs Predominantly in a Social Context

Behaviour which is acceptable to the culture and social group of the parents is rewarded. Behaviour which is not acceptable to the parents is blocked by the withholding of rewards, or by punishment; that is, by interposing social barriers to such behaviour.

Thus physical needs give rise to a wide variety of derived or social needs which can be satisfied only in socially approved ways. A young child learns to avoid feelings of anxiety and rejection which arise when his goal-striving is frustrated, by adapting his behaviour to the demands of his parents or teachers on whom he depends for need satisfaction. If he perceives them as loving and need-satisfying, he will love them; imitate and strive continually to maintain a feeling of security and of being accepted. Since he experiences few frustrations in this type of environment, he will probably enjoy mental health.

But if his goal-seeking activity is frequently rebuffed without reasons being made clear or alternates made possible, or if he is praised on one occasion and punished on another for the same thing, the child will behave defensively, and experience feelings of anxiety. Because of his physical inferiority the child will usually repress feelings of hostility towards parents and other figures of authority, and submit passively to their demands. Some children may become openly rebellious, and fight against this felt injustice by defiance. Repressed hostility may find its outlet in the destruction of toys, bullying other children, cruelty to animals, and other forms of

33

behaviour that are socially unacceptable, and more difficult to discover.

In early childhood, the culture pattern of any society is transmitted to children directly through the immediate family group—mother, father, brothers and sisters. By accepting the training they impose, the child will conform to the pattern of behaviour or social role which his group expects of him. The type of behaviour approved by the family group is in turn directly influenced by the particular social class to which they belong or wish to belong.

In some classes of our society, traits such as cleanliness, honesty, politeness, and correct form of speech, are highly valued and the parental attitudes towards these types of behaviour are accepted by the child as his own. In other social classes, different sets of values or attitudes may be stressed. In a family where 'bad' language, intemperance, physical aggression, immorality, and dishonesty are not only approved, but practised by the family group, the child will probably accept these values and will conform to this type of behaviour, except where, as in the classroom, it is safer to accept a different set of standards. A child from the former family group will have a set of attitudes, values, and social needs different from those of a child in the latter social group. The family background is thus an important factor in understanding the behaviour of any child. So, in any situation, the child will usually experience a need to conform to the behaviour expected of him in this situation by his in-group, rather than that expected by some out-group.

Example. A child who uses bad grammar in every-day speech may be repeating the language which he continually uses at home. His language at school may even be an improvement on that used at home, but still not up to the standard required by the school. Correct forms of speech may in fact be ridiculed by his parents and, as a consequence, be avoided by the child in his striving for parental affection.

Self-esteem—How its Development Influences Behaviour

The differentiation of 'self' from the rest of the environment begins in early infancy. The feeling of self is important since it is the point of reference for all one's behaviour. The value a person places on himself is determined by the extent to which he feels himself to be an accepted, participating member of a group.

The Social Conditions for Successful Learning

If the child's needs, both physical and social, are adequately satisfied by the family group, he puts a high value on his self-esteem. He will in all probability strive to maintain and enhance this value by conforming to their demands, and he may consider himself to be a good child, or a wanted child. Conversely, if he feels that he is rejected by the group on whom he depends for security and acceptance, feelings of anxiety arise, and his behaviour will be motivated towards defending rather than enhancing his self-esteem.

At the pre-kindergarten stage, the most important, and in some cases the only, social groups in which the child participates are within the family circle. How well his needs are satisfied by his family has an important bearing on the type of adjustment he will later make to other groups.

Problems of adjustment depend upon the extent to which the child's valuation of himself, derived from the family group, differs from that accorded him by other groups. A good example is the problem that arises when a child is overprotected or indulged by his parents.

Everything the child does appears to please them; he is seldom if ever restricted in his behaviour, and as a consequence he develops the feeling 'I am a very good boy'. He has no clearly defined limits of behaviour, and to the extent that his behaviour is unrestricted, he will be insecure. When he moves from the family group to the play group of his own age, he finds that his status in the family group is considerably higher than that accorded him by his peer group. In attempting to maintain his inflated self-esteem he behaves as he does in the home situation by demanding his own way, and refusing to conform to the co-operative behaviour demanded by his peer group. As a result he is usually rejected by them. His need for acceptance on terms commensurate with his self-esteem is frustrated, and he will behave defensively—by refusing to participate in their activities —or sulk, or be aggressive, or even withdraw from the group. He may attempt to enter into another, usually younger group, where he may be accepted at his own evaluation.

In the school situation, rejection by his peers may lead him to strive to maintain the value he has placed on himself by 'toadying' to the teacher, attempting to focus attention on himself by self-imposed monitorial duties with the obvious intention of becoming a 'teacher's pet' as he is the family pet. If these methods fail, he will try others—usually physical domination, bribery by lollies or other subterfuges. The teacher's acceptance of him at his own valuation forces him farther out of the peer group. Moreno sociograms (see Chapter 4) frequently show that if a 'teacher's pet' exists in a grade, he is strongly rejected by most of his peers.

When the self-esteem derived from the family group is comparable with that derived from other groups, the child can conform to the behaviour expected by his group without a feeling of threat to his self-esteem. On the one hand, he may experience a feeling of equality among members. Then his need for security within the group is satisfied, because there exists a feeling of mutual dependence between himself and other group members. His need to maintain and enhance his self-esteem will be achieved through co-operative activities towards mutually acceptable goals.

On the other hand, if he perceives himself to be superior in status in specific tasks to other group members, and he is accepted at this level by the group, he will function as a leader, and his self-esteem will be maintained or enhanced by leading group activity toward the group goals.

Another problem occurs when a child's early attempts at maintaining his self-esteem have been met with restrictions, ridicule, rejection, and over-critical attacks by his family. This results in an undervaluation of himself. He becomes cowed and his needs change from enhancement to defence.

This undervaluation of himself carries over to the school. He continues to approach every task with an expectation of failure, not because of his poor potentialities, but because he accepts himself as a failure. He adapts to this perception of himself by selecting as his peers other children who are considered failures by figures of authority (parents and teachers), or younger children who will be functioning at a level equivalent to his own.

Similarly a child who is well adjusted at home, but who consistently fails in academic work, or who is subjected to restrictions which he feels to be unjust, to ridicule, social rejection, and over-critical attacks may readjust his reactions and learning to the level accorded him by the teacher, or he may join in groups which are in actual or symbolic rebellion against the teacher.

The Social Conditions for Successful Learning

Give a child a bad name often enough, and he will rebel in defence of his self-esteem, or sink into passive submission.

The Classroom

The physical objects of the classroom differ very little among schools. The dais, the table, the rows of desks, the blackboard and the uncovered wooden floors do not usually change much during the period of formal learning.

Many teachers appreciate that such an environment has limitations and make serious and often successful attempts to transform the essentially drab classroom by introducing colour and attractively designed teaching aids. This is particularly noticeable in the infant departments of most primary schools, where emphasis on colour, music, and activity provides an atmosphere of interest and exciting adventure for the rapidly developing child. At this stage children are usually found to have a genuine liking for school. Indeed, in congested and under-privileged districts of any city, school holidays are regarded with disfavour by children in kindergarten or infant departments.

When the child reaches the age of eight years (usually after three years at school), he passes to the middle department of the school. Here he becomes increasingly separated from the attractive environment of the infant department. The exciting adventures with scissors, pastels, plasticine, and music become things of the past, and a more sober and serious demeanour is required.

Here the child learns to sit on a hard seat, not to move, scrape his feet, or gaze out of the window. He learns to *listen*, to answer questions by raising his hand, to draw neat red lines in a book and write or script-print on a single blue line in *exactly* the same way as *all* his peers. He may be permitted to ask questions, but for the most part, he is expected to conform. The teacher teaches, the child listens. He soon appreciates the advantages of conformity. He realizes that deviation is unprofitable and can lead to attacks (usually social) on his evaluation of himself. Thus the emphasis changes from eager participation and enthusiasm for new tasks to conformity with new roles imposed by the 'big school'.

Any grade of pupils is made up of a number of friendship groups, and not of isolated individuals. These groups exist because they

37

satisfy the need for security through group membership, and through them children practise social living.

Needs of the Teacher

An examination of the needs of the teacher may enable one to understand more fully the way in which he perceives the classroom. His behaviour in the school situation may be considered as being determined by his needs:

(*a*) to deserve promotion by getting a good teaching assessment and the approval of his superiors;

(*b*) to be accepted by his own peer group, which includes his head teacher or principal;

(*c*) to be accepted by his pupils so that they will willingly accept as theirs the goals which he helps to set for them;

(*d*) and to obtain the co-operation of the parents of his pupils so that the school goals may be supported at home.

He must instruct his pupils in a variety of subjects, and his advancement in his profession is often largely dependent on the facility his pupils acquire in academic subjects and in a rather narrow range of social skills.

How the Teacher sees the Classroom

Every teacher will see the classroom differently. Many teachers attempt to see the classroom as being composed of a number of separate individuals. They know that between certain pupils there are bonds of friendship. However, they sometimes assess these friendship groups as detrimental to good discipline. The teacher's efforts may then be directed at breaking up such friendship groups and isolating individuals, so that they have only individual pupils to instruct without the distracting effects of the social needs of the child.

The motivation of these children will be towards the satisfaction of the needs which arise from their group membership, in spite of the restrictions imposed by the teacher. They may use tricks and subterfuges to do this, and in general will not be motivated towards scholastic achievement.

Other teachers, however, will also see these friendship groups but will use them as a means to achieving both their immediate ends and the more general end of education: the development of a rounded personality.

The Needs of the Child

Children attend school for a number of reasons, first to obey the laws of society, and later also to satisfy their own personal needs. From the social point of view, schools are necessary to equip children with skills which will enable them eventually to play an adult role and so perpetuate the culture pattern. The school is thus a socializing agent of culture. But this long-range goal is so remote that few, if any, children could experience a need to attend school merely for this reason.

So as to ensure that children are adequately trained to fulfil the needs of society, they are legally compelled to attend school for a specific period, usually from their sixth to their fourteenth or fifteenth years. Most children are aware of the consequences which result from truancy, and some may experience a need to attend school merely to avoid the consequences.

Apart from the legal aspects of compulsory attendance, most children want to attend school because they feel a need to widen their experiences through social contact with other children. But the excitement of many a little child whose school bag is packed some days beforehand in eager anticipation of the first day at school almost invariably gives way to feelings of anxiety and insecurity during the first few days of school life, when he is confronted with an entirely new situation, in many ways quite different from the one anticipated. Perhaps he had not thought what it would be like to leave mother at the gate, or whether the other children, or the teacher, would like him until he found himself in the real situation at school.

A child who is emotionally well adjusted in his pre-school life readjusts fairly quickly to this new situation, and once he has found membership in a play group among children of his own age, and has won the approval of his teacher, his anxiety diminishes and his feeling of security extends from the home to the school. The school then provides situations both in the classroom and in the playground in which feelings of self-confidence can be enhanced.

In an attempt to retain and strengthen the feelings of social acceptance and security derived from school groups, he will conform to the type of behaviour expected of him, and, provided he is of average intelligence, he will approach new learning confidently, and will respond to encouragement and praise by increased effort. But the child who is not well adjusted emotionally tends to be more highly prone to anxiety in new or unfamiliar situations, and consequently tries to avoid them.

The anxiety experienced in his early school life is more intense and more prolonged than that of most other children. During this period of maladjustment it is not uncommon for the behaviour of such a child to regress to an earlier stage of development. Thumb-sucking, lisping, crying at the least upset, and choosing as playmates children who are much younger than himself are common reactions of this type of child. Lacking confidence, his initial attempts at formal learning invariably result in failure, and in turn increase his anxiety.

A child who is emotionally very disturbed, and who is punished by those responsible for his training, or is teased by other children, may react in a variety of ways—by withdrawing further into himself or by defiance, bullying, or destructiveness, and refusing to attempt school work.

Although this sort of behaviour may appear to be irrational, it is, from his point of view, the most effective way he knows to give expression to the tensions arising from the frustration of his demanding needs for affection, acceptance, and security. Merely punishing such behaviour without attempting to remove the underlying cause, serves only to increase his feelings of insecurity and to intensify his anxiety. In many cases it will lead to other, more serious forms of anti-social behaviour. If one type of behaviour such as thumb-sucking is checked without consideration as to its cause, other activities less obvious, but more disturbing to the child's later adjustment will be resorted to in an attempt to allay the anxiety aroused by his frustrated needs.

Whereas the well-adjusted child will experience a need to do well at school work, and try to gain greater prestige, the insecure child's most pressing need may be to defend himself against further feelings of rejection by others. Under the disturbing influence of this need his chances of learning new skills become seriously impaired. Restlessness, poor concentration, day-dreaming, and, in situations of greater tension, defiance, aggression, and jealousy are symptomatic of the emotional disturbance caused by the thwarting of his basic needs for acceptance, security and affection.

Unless the insecure child receives sympathetic and patient guidance by understanding parents and teachers, he will find it increasingly difficult to adjust to social situations. The child who tends to be unpopular with other children soon becomes the scapegoat, and the teasing he gets will greatly intensify his feelings of insecurity, and seriously disturb his emotional and social development.

How the Pupil sees the Classroom

Each pupil sees the classroom differently. His impressions are derived from his experience with other children. Depending on his position relative to other children, he may see himself as a member of one or more groups, as a leader of a group on occasions, as the leader in the classroom, or as being rejected by most or all of the children's groups. Sociometric studies (see Chapter 4) have shown that most children in the classroom see other children and themselves as members of little friendship groups, who prefer to play together in the playground and try to sit near each other in school. They know, in most cases, why the children are members of their particular group—'They live near each other'—'They are all in the football team'. They can name the leaders as well as those who are not accepted as members of any groups, and say why they are in these social positions.

The child who tends to be rejected by groups of children sees the group formations more distinctly than do other children who are members of a closely knit group, because he has at various times attempted to satisfy his need for security by trying to enter one or other group.

The child sees the classroom as a functioning group with various sub-groups, of which he is or is not a participating member. If he is a participating member of a group he will have security in the group and will strive to enhance his self-esteem within the group regulations by striving towards the group goals, and assisting other members to achieve the goals (if he is able to do this). Thus he learns to exercise initiative.

However, if he is not able to become a member of a group, he will not feel secure and accepted, and while he strives to obtain membership of some group all other goals will fall into the background. In that case there will be regression to earlier forms of behaviour that tended to satisfy the need for security, or rebellious defiance of other children, and the rules of social and ethical conduct of the society. The children see the teacher as either a need-satisfying or need-frustrating adult, while they themselves play mostly subordinate roles.

Motivation in the Classroom—The Problem of the Conflict of Needs

All children at some time or another find themselves in conflict situations which arouse feelings of anxiety. It can be shown that feelings of anxiety can be reduced to a minimum provided some type of communication with other people is established. A teacher who is sensitive to this need for expression will provide situations wherein the curriculum subjects can be used to give expression to this anxiety. Subjects such as Art and English Expression are especially suitable for this purpose.

However, if the needs of a child are denied expression in the classroom, he will be in a conflict situation, and will be unable to carry out the imposed tasks at the highest level of his ability.

Inattention, poor concentration, and day-dreaming may result from his attempts to resolve the conflict.

It is possible, for example, that a child may be worried about his mother who is seriously ill in hospital. During the Art lesson he could be given the opportunity to express his feelings of anxiety freely through colour and form of his own choice, or he could, like the others, be required to draw a flower pot. The first will reduce his anxiety; the second will prevent him from satisfying either his own or the teacher's needs. His anxiety will be increased as he is forced to suppress his own need for personal expression, and consequently he will fail miserably in the performance of the imposed task.

All teachers know of children who are not interested, day-dream, and cannot concentrate. Many ruses or spurs are used in attempts to overcome this unacceptable behaviour. Teachers make their teaching more intrinsically interesting by using visual aids, less formal teaching, and more pupil activity. When these methods fail to arouse the desired response, they use social spurs such as continued oral questioning, or highlighting the behaviour by verbal attack on the pupil. These methods at best give limited success, and may increase the conflict. This unsatisfactory state of affairs can be overcome by the child's participation in group activities aimed at a group goal. This will satisfy the need for security, communication and enhancement of the self. These are such strong needs that other needs external to the school situation may be momentarily forgotten because of increased involvement in the school task.

Motivation in the Classroom—The Problem of Goal Setting

All molar behaviour is goal-seeking activity for the purpose of need satisfaction. The major problem of the classroom is to set goals that are mutually acceptable to both teacher and pupils. Therefore, all goals must be meaningfully related to the existing needs of the group as perceived by teachers and children.

The teacher in his intermingled roles of instructor, trainer in social habits, and inculcator of ethical precepts should function as a leader in goal setting.

If a goal is too remote, it is not clearly enough perceived, and activity ceases unless a substitute goal is introduced. If the goals are set from the teacher's point of view, the danger exists that these goals may be unrelated to the children's existing needs. For instance, the teacher may believe that children ought to feel the need to pass examinations so that they may attain enhanced status in an adult community later; but the goal as seen by the teacher, and the methods necessary to attain this goal, may be beyond the comprehension of the young child. Spontaneous activity on the part of the child in the direction of the imposed goal will diminish, and the teacher will feel impelled to introduce artificial incentives to increase the motivation towards the long-range goal.

These artificial or indirect incentives may be:

(*a*) marks gained by competition between individual children,

(*b*) corporal punishment,

(*c*) verbal attack, and

(*d*) the most potent negative incentive of all, a threat to the children's immediate social needs of security within the peer group and the need for communication.

When barriers to communication arise, tensions increase between teacher and child, and between children. One effect of this is the emotional rejection of new learning which is indicated by poor retention and positive forgetting. The need to enhance self-esteem is then replaced by a need to defend it. The child attempts to do this by accepting for himself a level of aspiration below his capacity level with a consequent decrease in the level of his performance. This may be called 'the problem of under-production'.

Under-production occurs when a pupil's attainment is lower than his general ability level would lead one to expect. Most teachers can indicate a few children in their classes who 'could do better'. They are not usually aware that in permissive social conditions, the production level of even the 'dullards' may be raised to a relatively high level; and that of the bright pupil dramatically increased in scope and standard. Goal-setting should be directly related both to the immediate social needs of the children, and to the more remote goal of adjustment in the adult community.

Goal-setting should meet the following requirements:

(*a*) Satisfaction of the need for security within a social group. This can be effected by allowing mutually selected sub-groups to be formed (see Chapters 4–6) so that barriers to communication between the pupils and between pupils and teacher are reduced to a minimum.

(*b*) The range of mental ability in a sub-group must be such that there is no great disparity between the level of aspiration of the sub-group and the capacity of its individual members.

(*c*) The teacher must function for the group as the accepted leader in intellectual skills. To do this, he must relinquish his authoritarian role and eliminate the children's perception of him as a threat to their self-esteem.

(*d*) Competition between individual children should be replaced by co-operative effort towards group goals. Competition between groups of children can be used sparingly as a motivating force provided there are also constant opportunities for co-operation.

In order to eliminate any threat to the self-esteem in any group, thought should be given to the integration of all minor group activities in the class effort.

Lippitt and White (6) in an experimental study on leadership and group life have demonstrated the significant effects of differing social climates on levels of performance and types of behaviour. The implications of this study have an important bearing on the problem of goal-setting in the classroom.

In the democratic social climate, in which group members participated in goal-setting, there was a marked increase in initiative, co-operation, and work-minded conversation. Fewer frustrations and a marked decrease in aggressive behaviour towards the leader are also recorded. In the *laissez-faire* group, in which the leader did not participate in the setting of goals, production was at a minimum, and much activity was directed towards non-productive goals.

The most effective method, as shown by the above experiment, is that in which both the teacher and pupils are functioning members of the one group.

In the democratic classroom, the children participate in goal-setting under the leadership of the teacher. He is thus a participant member of the child group, but, because of his superiority in age, skill, and experience, he functions as a leader and influences group decisions. Because he is an accepted member of the group, the need for communication between group members is facilitated, tensions between children tend to disappear, producing a tremendous release of energy which is used in the attainment of group goals. The need for the teacher to maintain discipline and to boost the productive level of his pupils by introducing indirect incentives disappears, since the goals set are related to the immediate social needs of both the teacher and the children. Non-conforming behaviour by any individual member results in censure by the group, and many disciplinary problems are handled by the children themselves.

Under such conditions, in which self-esteem is not threatened, and suitable opportunities for its enhancement are provided, the level of aspiration rises by itself, without having to be artificially boosted.

Ethical Precepts and Motivation

Children who copy, tell lies, steal, are disobedient, or who are defiant, are frequently regarded by the teacher as 'bad' children. But a teacher faced with such conduct is frequently at a loss to understand the behaviour or to know what action would be most appropriate. Both he and the child realize that the behaviour is partly unintentional. Severe punishments, even when increased on repetition of the offence, are not usually effective. Such children are motivated towards goals which are not socially approved in the school situation. It may well be that this conduct is approved and in fact practised by the family group. The child, having accepted the family values, feels that the type of behaviour expected of him by the teacher is incompatible with that approved by his family. The teacher's goals are unreal to him, and the spurs imposed by the teacher appear to him to be unwarranted. The rebellion, as exemplified in his anti-social conduct, is against the enforcement of rules which are unreal and meaningless to him. The child is not motivated therefore towards what the teacher calls 'good' conduct. The punishment he has received reinforces his feelings of resentment towards the teacher and is expressed in his attempts to outwit the teacher at every opportunity.

Such a child tends to be an isolate in the classroom or a member of a small isolated 'gang' and to remain so unless encouraged to participate in the attainment of class goals. The child will devote his whole attention towards doing the things that are banned by the teacher, while at the same time attempting to avoid the consequences of his anti-social behaviour. This type of behaviour, motivated as it is towards outwitting authority and breaking rules without discovery, has implications which extend beyond the classroom into all aspects of adult life. The crucial problem in preventing the development of this anti-social motivation, is how to provide children with opportunities for participation in the formulation of social rules which are mutually acceptable to the group members, and which are compatible with the requirements of society.

SELECTED REFERENCES FOR FURTHER READING

1. SNYGG, D. and COMBS, A. N., *Individual Behaviour* (New York. Harper, 1949). Recommended as a reference book for expanding this chapter.
2. STREADER, D. C., 'But do the children learn', 1949. (Unpublished B.Ed., thesis held at the School of Education, University of Melbourne.) An evaluation of the North Brunswick Experiment. Shows that this 'activity method' school achieved the educational goals to Grade VI level better than similar but more orthodox schools.

The Social Conditions for Successful Learning

3. PRESTON, M. G., and HEINTZ, R. K., 'Effects of Participation *vs* Supervisory Leadership on Group Judgment', *J. Abn. and Social Psychol.*, **44**, 1949, 345–55. Shows how the participant group leader and his group received more satisfaction in doing the task than the supervisory leader and his group, and retained the group decisions as their own.

4. BENJAMINS, J., 'Changes in Performance in Relation to Influences upon Self-conceptualization', *J. Abn. and Social Psychol.*, **45**, 1950, 473–80. Shows by an experiment that an individual continually seeks to establish or maintain an identity by which to conceptualize himself and thus arrive at his role in a given situation. This identity must be compatible with other evidence—if it is to make sense (p. 479).

   Reported (i.e. false) IQ's on a test affected results on the parallel form of the test in the way predicted from the individual's attempts to readjust his concept of himself as a result of the first 'reported' IQ.

5. COCH, L., and FRENCH, J. R. P. Junr., 'Overcoming Resistance to Change', *Hum. Rel.*, **1**, 1948, 512–32. The authors showed experimentally that a democratic permissive atmosphere of group participation and freedom of communication effects changes in job methods and production levels, and is superior to the more autocratic method whereby change in methods and new production levels in a factory are determined by the management.

   BARKER, KOUNIN and WRIGHT (Editors), *Child Behaviour and Development* (New York, McGraw-Hill, 1943). Chapter XXVII—'Domination and Socially Integrative Behaviour'. Anderson, H. H., 459–83. Compares a democratic with an authoritarian teacher in terms of progress and personality development of the children. Chapter XVIII—The 'Social Climate of Children's Groups'. Lippitt, R., and White, R. K. Shows that a democratic social climate is accompanied by high morale, freer communication, more friendships, less discontent and aggressive behaviour, and greater organized play, than is the authoritarian social climate.

7. THELEN, H. A., and WITHALL, JOHN, 'Three Frames of Reference— The Description of Climate', *Hum. Rel.*, **2**, 1949, 159–76. Shows that a good deal of the teacher's time in a teacher-centred (autocratic) climate is wasted in directing and reproving his pupils, with the net effect of antagonizing them.

8. MOSS, H. A. (Ed.) *Comparative Psychology* (New York, Prentice Hall Inc. 1942). Chapter 4 (Motivation) and Chapter 13 (Social Behaviour of Animals) describe studies of animal behaviour and show that adaptive behaviour such as group play, co-operativeness, and communication, are essential to social life in animals.

9. HARRIMAN, PHILIP L. (Ed.), *Twentieth Century Psychology* (New York, The Philosophical Library, 1946). Several chapters in this book are relevant, but in particular: *Training in Democratic Leadership*. Bavelas,

Alex and Lewin, Kurt, 175–81. Shows how morale (increased self-esteem through satisfaction) increased greatly under leaders who used democratic methods. *Patterns of Aggressive Behaviour in Experimentally Created Social Climates*. Lewin, Kurt; Lippitt, Ronald and White, Ralph K. 200–29. Shows that patterns of aggression, domination, and submission differ in autocratic, democratic, and *laissez-faire* social climates (boys' clubs). 'In the first experiment, hostility was thirty times as frequent in the autocratic as in the democratic group.' 'In the second experiment, four "autocratic" groups showed an apathetic pattern of behaviour.'

10. KRECH, D., and CRUTCHFIELD, RICHARD S., *Theory and Problems of Social Psychology* (New York, McGraw-Hill, 1948). A more advanced text book on motivation, perception, attitudes, and other problems of social psychology.

11. NEWCOMB, T. M., and HARTLEY, G. L. *et al.*, *Readings in Social Psychology* (New York, Holt, 1947), revised edn., 1952. This is an indispensable reference book for those who wish to read more widely in the whole field of social psychology. All the points made in this and other chapters concerning social processes and their effects on behaviour will be found greatly expanded and illustrated.

12. CHILD, IRVIN L., and WHITING, W. M., 'Determinants of Level of Aspiration Evidence from Everyday Life', *J. Abn. and Social Psychol.*, **44**, 1949, 303–14. Shows how success leads to striving for greater success, and how failure leads to a reduction in the striving for success

13. SCHWEBEL, MILTON, and ASCH, MORTON, J. 'Research Possibilities in Non-directive Teaching'. *J. Educ. Psychol.*, **39**, 1948, 359–69. 'The basic task in motivation is in stimulating the drive to growth and development. The accomplishment of the student is directly related to the degree of freedom afforded him and his readiness to accept it' (p. 368).

14. DEUTSCH, MORTON., 'An Experimental Study of the Effects of Co-operation and Competition upon Group Process', *Hum. Rel.*, **2**, 1949, 199–231. Shows the social, educational, and individual advantages of co-operation.

15. SUTTIE, IAN D., *The Origins of Love and Hate* (London, Kegan Paul, 1945). Deals with importance of love and affection for the development of children.

16. CARMICHAEL, L. (Ed.), *Manual of Child Psychology* (New York, Wiley, 1946). Chapter 10, 'Language Development in Children'. McCarthy, Dorothea, 476–568. Points out the increasing interest in the social function of language in a child's life. Chapter 14, 'Character Development in Children—An Objective Approach'. Jones, Vernon, 707–48. Outlines researches on the forces inducing character development—both inherited and environmental. Note especially the effect of group membership. Chapter 16, 'Behaviour and Development as a

48

Function of the Total Situation'. Lewin, Kurt, 791–840. Outlines forces operating in the situation. Note especially sections on conflict and changes in needs and goals.

17. MURPHY, MURPHY, and NEWCOMB, *Experimental Social Psychology* (New York, Harper, 1937). Chapter III. 'The Biology of Motives'. Note especially the section on 'The Theory of Adience'. Chapter IV, 'The Learning Process in Social Situations'.
18. WITHALL, J., 'The Development of a Technique for the Measurement of Social Emotional Climate in Classrooms', *J. Exp. Educ.*, **17**, 1949, 347–62.
19. BONNEY, MERL E., 'A Study of the Sociometric Process among Sixth Grade Children', *J. Educ. Psychol.*, **37**, 1946, 359–72. Assimilation of status groups into society—play activities.
20. BILLINGLEA, F. Y. and BLOOM, H., 'The Comparative Effect of Frustration and Success on Goal Directed Behaviour', *J. Abn. and Social Psychol.*, **45**, 1950, 510–15. Shows how frustration tends to lead to less work, and more attempts at adjustment to the situation.

IV

The Classroom as a Social Group

O. A. OESER

Synopsis

FEW books discuss the implications for education of not having one teacher to each pupil. The traditional classroom, in which the teacher requires pupils to attend only to him, implies that each teacher has one pupil, to whom, however, he devotes only a fraction of class time. Since this is in conflict with the actual facts of social organization within the classroom, this chapter will discuss the psychological structure of the classroom. The following two chapters will then show how some of these principles can be applied to the provision of better opportunities for the potentialities of the child.

THE CLASSROOM AS A FIELD OF SOCIAL INTERACTIONS[1]

The implications of social structure in a classroom. Any group of people will display patterns of interaction. Each person affects every other and some, usually described as 'leaders', influence the behaviour of the members of a group more than others.

As every teacher knows, and as a sociogram (Chapter 5) will quickly demonstrate, the classroom group is no exception. It will

---

[1] This section owes much to discussions with S. B. Hammond and G. B. Sharp.

comprise several sub-groups or cliques. Sometimes the pupil who most influences the group is neither the obvious one nor the one chosen by the teacher.

Three of the most important social problems of the educator are: to turn the latent leadership of a group in the direction of the educational process; to encourage the individual development of leadership; and to encourage co-operative striving towards common goals while discouraging the exercise of authoritarian leadership. Looked at in a wider frame of reference, these are also the problems of creating active citizenship. If citizenship is not to begin in the classroom, where is it to begin? An intellectual course in social studies is no substitute for practical experience and all the personal and emotional involvement which the word 'practical' entails.

Since every classroom contains groups or cliques, it seems reasonable to use this fact. If a teacher can get groups to work together, he effectively increases the number of pupils whom he can teach, or, if this statement seems paradoxical, he effectively increases the intensity of his teaching. Whenever he helps a group, his teaching is disseminated, discussed, and practised through that group, especially if it has felt a need for information or help.

LEARNING FROM AUTHORITY

Every teacher knows that 'he learns from his pupils' when they ask him questions which require him to give a careful analysis and explanation of fundamental principles. He frequently finds that he had simply learnt something (e.g. a principle in physics, or a statement about the motives of an historical character) by accepting someone's word for its being so. In other words, there is a strong tendency to accept statements on authority without examining the evidence. This is true of children as well as of adults.

If a person accepts statements on authority without thinking about them and integrating them with the rest of his knowledge, he tends to learn them by rote and to forget them as easily as he accepted them. This is most obvious in mathematics but is true of all subjects.

Conversely, even adults often lack the courage to express doubts or to admit ignorance when face to face with authority. But they will do so among their friends and equals. This important social fact is the basis of forming groups in a classroom and allowing free discussion among their members. If a teacher can succeed in encouraging a sense of freedom in the approach to knowledge (or truth), his pupils will learn better and become more flexible. In other words, they will early acquire that willingness to learn and to accept something new which is characteristic of the scientific attitude.

But to be effective in this sense, discussion must take place between equals. If the teacher wishes his pupils to learn through active participation, he must allow them to argue with each other, to work with each other, and so to learn to tolerate each other's weaknesses and strengths. In doing this, he may himself have to learn to tolerate criticism, and to view objectively his own strengths and weaknesses.

The process of group structuring in the classroom. There are many forms of interaction between teacher and pupils, and between pupils. Each form will be appropriate to a given task, will satisfy (or express) a particular need. It cannot be said, therefore, that any one form is the best in all circumstances. It will be appropriate now to inspect the major types of interaction which occur.

Suppose a new teacher comes into the class for the first time and starts teaching a new subject.

Situation 1. *The Lecture. Passive Learning.* In this situation the

FIGURE 1

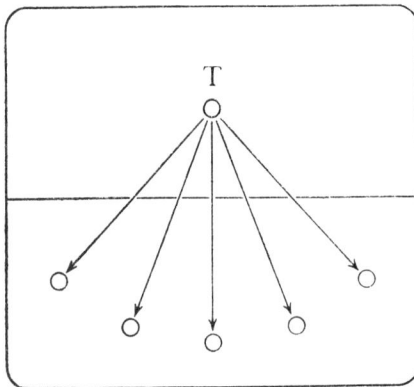

teacher speaks, the pupils listen and there is no interaction between the pupils. Moreover, the interaction between pupils and teacher is confined to the processes of listening, perceiving, and assimilating. It is typical of this situation that the teacher makes statements. He may ask occasional questions, but he sets the pace even though he may adapt his pace to that of the slower members of the class.

This situation occurs not only in the talk or lecture, where it is inevitable, but in many other cases. When the situation is that of a lecture, it is expected and accepted by the audience, which will sometimes itself deal with noisy members; but if it occurs regularly in a classroom, the pupils' experience is one of coercion and the role of the teacher is not altogether dissimilar to that of the sergeant-major or policeman. There is a sharp distinction (indicated by the line across Fig. 1) between teacher and class.

This situation, then, may be characterized as *teacher-centred, task directed, autocratic with passive learning.*

Situation 2. *Emergence of Leadership. The lecture-discussion.* Here the teacher encourages the pupils to ask questions freely. The arrows

FIGURE 2

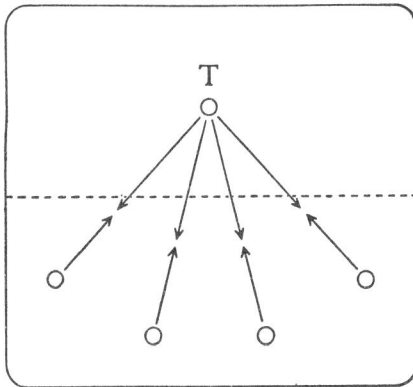

indicate that there is continuous interchange of verbal behaviour between teacher and pupils. He assumes the role and responsibilities of leading the children. He asks leading questions. He gives answers to the questions of individual pupils and gets answers from individual pupils. In this situation there will be competition between pupils who

53

give the right answers or who want to catch the teacher's eye. The teacher's role is that of the hierarchical leader. Other examples would be the conductor of an orchestra, and any institutional leader. But in the classroom the initiative need not always be that of the teacher. The closed division between teacher and pupils shown in Fig. 1 now becomes a permeable division.

Hence this situation may be characterized as *teacher and task centred, autocratic, moving in the direction of co-operation and active learning.*

Situation 3. *Active Learning.* The dotted arrows here indicate that the teacher permits discussion between pupils who are allowed to

FIGURE 3

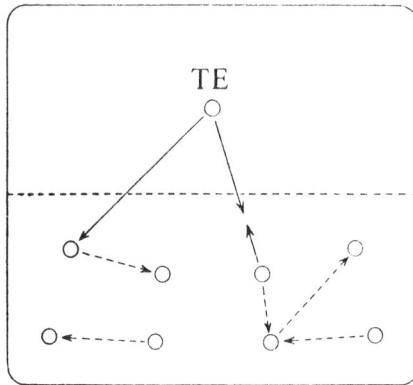

help each other. A common example is the science laboratory. The letters 'TE' at the top of the diagram are intended to indicate that the teacher now begins to assume also the role of 'expert' or of chairman. He, of course, retains his other roles as well; but the emphasis in the teaching process now fluctuates between the needs established by the task and the needs of the individual pupils.

This situation may, therefore, be characterized as being *task and pupil centred*, and to begin to have a *co-operative structure*.

Situation 4. *Active Learning; independent planning.* Here the social structure of the classroom has been radically changed. The pupils are active in small groups, preferably self-chosen (see Chapters 5 and 6) and the teacher now functions mainly in the role of *expert*

FIGURE 4

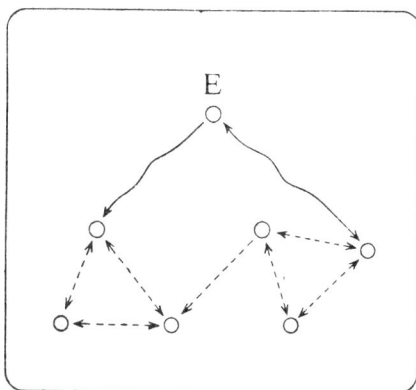

consultant. In this situation the groups map out their work, adapt to each other's pace, discuss their difficulties and agree on solutions. There is independent exploration, active learning, and a maximal development of task-directed leadership in each group. The wavy line in Fig. 4 indicates that at a particular time some conflict has arisen, or a difficulty has occurred which cannot be solved by that particular group. An appeal or a question is now directed to the teacher. His role is that of the expert and chief planner. The social climate is permissive and co-operative. It may, therefore, be characterized as *pupil and task centred*, and as having *pupil-syncratic structure*.

Situation 5. *The Discussion Group, Syndicate, Seminar.* This is the characteristic situation of a group which is dealing with a specific issue or problem, e.g. a working party or seminar. The arrows indicate that the group as a whole perceives a certain task and that, as in a debate, the verbal activities of the group are directed to the task itself, its elucidation, clarification, formulation, and solution.

Once again, therefore, this is a task-centred situation, but it differs radically from Situations 1 and 2 because of the absence of explicit hierarchical structure.

An example may make the point clearer. In Situation 4 a class is, say, working in small groups through a set of algebraic equations in the textbook. When any one group (or the class as a whole) finds one

FIGURE 5

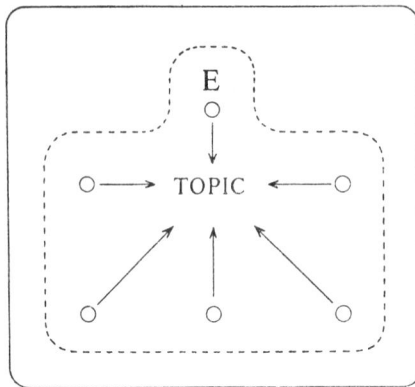

insoluble, the teacher is called in as an expert to give help and advice. But the work of the other groups proceeds, because the groups may be doing different exercises. In Situation 5, on the other hand, the group as a whole will be discussing some *topic*: for example, 'What is Algebra?' 'What is the Nature of Space?' 'How are the Theorems of Euclid related to each other?' 'Why does one have to start with Axioms, go on to Angles and then to Congruency?'

The more advanced the class is, the more often will this occur. In Situations 3 and 4 there may be preparatory work in the English class on the set play. At some stage, Situation 5 will arise, in which there is a general discussion of one of the 'characters' or of even more abstract topics such as 'style', or the difference between poetry and prose.

Ideally the role of the teacher here is simply that of a wise and experienced member of the group. His other roles which come into play to varying degrees in Situations 1–4, are merely latent. In a class that has been properly trained and is experienced in working together through small groups, the coercive teacher roles would hardly ever be activated; only in exceptional circumstances when some generalized excitement sweeps over the class will he have to be the autocrat or policeman.

Situation 5, then, may be characterized as being *group-task centred*, and having a *syncratic structure* (**1**).

56

The Classroom as a Social Group

The Relation between Situations 1–5

If, as in Fig. 6, these five situations are grouped together, it is clear

FIGURE 6

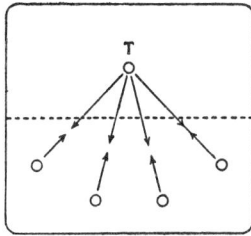

position 2

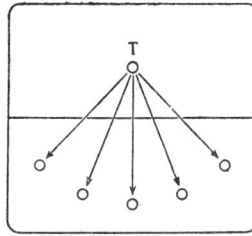

position 1

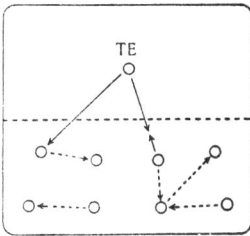

position 3

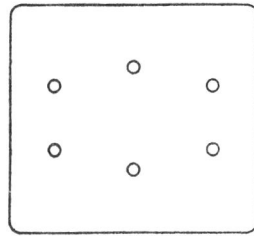

position 6

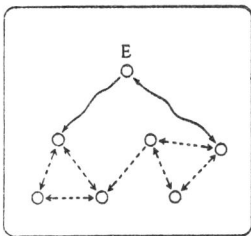

position 4

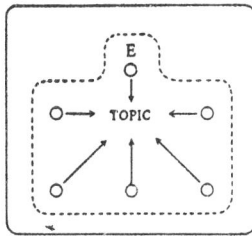

position 5

O. A. Oeser

that there is a progressive change from 1 to 5. It is also clear that at any given moment, a classroom could change from one to another, or revert to Situation 1, or to the new Situation 6 depicted in Fig. 6, where nothing happens. It is also clear that there must be transitional forms between each of these situations as well as some mixed forms when one of them initially breaks down. In teaching, of course, the last situation in Fig. 6 will occur only on special occasions such as examinations and the two minutes' silence on Armistice Day. It is, however, a situation and a type of group which is common in Group Therapy. But these transitional, mixed, and special forms will not be discussed here (2).

From Situations 1 to 4 there is a progressive change from teacher-centred through task-centred to pupil-centred activities, from passive to active learning, and from minimal to maximal participation, with a progressive diminution of the coerciveness of the teacher's roles. In Situation 5 the situation is again task-centred, but the teacher's status as such has disappeared.

Situation 1 in its pure form occurs only with a radio audience, for even in the lecture room there is some communication between lecturer and audience (signs of restlessness, applause and the like). It may be thought that as the size of the class grows, the 'lecture' situation would have to become dominant and that Situations 3–5 could occur only when the number is small, 5 being most efficient when the number of participants lies between two and ten. But even a large class of, say, fifty can be split up into groups and the teacher can move among them, so that instead of having to deal with fifty individuals, he can deal with five to ten groups.

A word of warning may not be out of place here. Situations 4, 5, and 6 cannot suddenly be created in a class that has been run on traditional (teacher-dominant) lines. They require careful preparation and training of the pupils by the teacher, who himself must expect to make mistakes but be prepared to acknowledge them (see Chapters 5 and 6).

The efficiency of situations. The question now is: Which of these classroom situations is the most efficient? Clearly, there is no simple answer to this question. Which situation should be encouraged will depend on the answer to the question 'efficiency for what?'; on the needs and the task of the moment; and on a number of other factors.

The Classroom as a Social Group

It is, however, of great importance that the teacher should be clearly aware of the sort of situation he is in, and why, and change it for reasons connected with the *task* and the changing needs of pupils, and not for reasons connected with his own status or need to be dominant.

In order to stimulate further thinking about and discussion of this topic, some of the major factors are set out below, without further comment.

Factors that define the situation

(1) High-low teacher dominance
(2) Large-small number of pupils
(3) High-low academic level of class
(4) Active-passive pupil participation
(5) Individual effort—co-operative effort
(6) Contentious-noncontentious material
(7) Long term—short term goals
(8) Clear-vague goals
(9) Strong-weak needs
(10) Task and learning oriented—examination oriented
(11) Directing-helping (counselling).

Discussion: Efficiency, anxiety and aggression, incentives and competition

In the classroom, Situations 1 and 2 are sometimes necessary: when some general instructions have to be given, or a method new to most is explained on the blackboard, or the teacher sums up the work of the groups and enables them to compare each other's work and findings. For other purposes, such situations are inefficient, since those who know are bored and many are inattentive for other reasons, thus compelling the teacher to waste energy in maintaining discipline. The other situations are far more efficient because they maintain the motivation of the pupils and, through repetition during discussion, increase the amount of practice during earning. Quite generally, leadership based on power or rank has been shown to be inefficient for learning, even in accepted hierarchical situations such as that of the army (3).

O. A. Oeser

In Situations 3, 4, and 5 other factors emerge, which both increase the efficiency of learning and contribute to the development of social maturity. Briefly, these are that through discussing and working together, pupils discover that they have

> similar difficulties;
> similar abilities;
> common, clearly defined aims;
> common achievements.

The effect of these repeatedly verified discoveries is to reduce anxiety, especially of those who are backward at the given task, and hence aggression. Everyone can achieve; his achievement is plain for his group to see; and the satisfactions of continuous achievement are not limited to the few.

In a team game, everyone co-operates, which by no means rules out competition among individuals to produce the best effort. The same is true of working in small groups in the classroom. Leadership is more evenly spread. Each group will have a leader, and the leader will be different for different tasks.

This point about accepted leadership can be put more generally. In a permissive social climate (as in Situations 3–5, unless the teacher has formed the groups by authoritarian fiat and continues to dominate each), leadership will express both a person's individual capacities and the needs of the group. Both the group leader and the teacher acquire authority through the sanction of the group. The difference between *authoritative* behaviour based on sanction or acceptance from the group, and *authoritarian* behaviour based on status or power is of crucial importance for the dynamics of a society, however small.

The more communication about ends and means there is between the members of a group, the more effective and efficient that group is likely to be. This has been amply demonstrated in many situations, especially in the Armed Forces and in Industry. In the present context, efficiency (or 'output') is measured by progress in learning. When a group clearly defines its goals and the means of reaching them, *and accepts both*, it has structured its immediate psychological future. Structuring the future reduces anxiety, which always accompanies uncertainty of structure; and reduced anxiety implies less

The Classroom as a Social Group

random behaviour (such as 'doodling' and day-dreaming), less aggression towards others, and less uncritical resistance to change.

Lastly, the teacher can dispense with spurious incentives, such as marks. Where marks are frequently given, pupils too often learn a task not because they want to or are interested, but because they do not want to appear as failures, or want to avoid criticism and punishment. In any large class, there is an upper quarter which usually gets the highest marks and a lower which usually comes bottom. Thus *for many pupils the experience of repeated failure is a dominant characteristic of their schooldays.*

An interesting and suggestive experiment is that of Deutsch (4). He matched two groups of schoolchildren for ability. One group solved tasks individually in a setting of high competitiveness, and the other was split into smaller co-operating groups. It was found that 'individualists' exhibited more destructive criticism than 'co-operators' (i.e., there was more aggression in the first case). Comparison of the two groups showed more of the following characteristics in the co-operative than in the competitive situation:

Co-ordination of effort
Diversity in amount of contribution per member
Subdivision of activity
Achievement pressure
Attentiveness to fellow members
Mutual comprehension of communication
Common appraisals of communication
Orientation and orderliness
Productivity per unit time
Quality of product and of discussions
Friendliness during discussions
Favourable evaluation of the group and its products
Perception of favourable effects on fellow members.

The group or syndicate method thus minimizes the experience of failure and increases the positive experience of co-operative success. All these findings have clear implications for the growth of social maturity (5)

O. A. Oeser

While traditional teaching methods overemphasize the individual as a lonely striver after knowledge or technical competence, the group methods suggested in this and the two following chapters could overemphasize the dependence of people on each other. The first makes the setting of standards of achievement a personal matter, a training in 'character'. It emphasizes the will. (Extracts from school reports: 'John *must concentrate* harder'; 'Mary could do better if she *tried* or *wanted to*'.) The second tends to make the person try because the others are trying and he does not want to be left out.

To resolve the dilemma between what Riesman (6) has called 'inner-directed' and 'other-directed' standards of social and intellectual behaviour is one of the problems each teacher must face. A theoretical exposition would be beyond the scope of this book, since it would require a discussion of generalized motivation and learning theories in relation to various types of individually defined and socially defined roles and purposes, ends and means.

This book assumes that neither the pure individualist nor the pure herd-man is a desirable citizen. Thus, the teacher should use 'group' methods of structuring the classroom to develop co-operation and eliminate factors extraneous to the goals of teaching, such as authoritarianism, sense of isolation, inability to formulate personal or group goals. He should use 'individual' methods to test individual achievement and to help the individual to get into the habit of setting and attaining his own standards or goals.

The five 'situations' of this chapter, then, are meant to be used flexibly and to be adapted to the needs of the class as a whole or to those of individuals as occasion demands. Every teacher who sincerely tries to use and to understand the psychology of these situations will become more pupil-centred and less self-centred. His pupils will understand, appreciate, and even on occasion demand his reverting from methods that stress co-operation among pupils to methods which stress the authority and knowledge of the teacher, since they will have learnt and understood the difference between a coercive and a directive situation.

The Classroom as a Social Group

SELECTED REFERENCES FOR FURTHER READING

1. For detailed theoretical discussions of the term syncratic see OESER, O. A., and HAMMOND S. B. (eds.), *Social Structure and Personality in a City* (London, Routledge & Kegan Paul, 1954).
2. Figures 1–5 are simplifications for ease of exposition: strictly, they should be drawn as topological diagrams, showing regions, boundaries, barriers and forces acting in each situation. *Vide* LEWIN, K., *Principles of Topological Psychology* (New York and London, McGraw-Hill, 1936).
3. KELLY, H. H., 'Communications in Experimentally Created Hierarchies', *Hum. Rel.*, **4**, 1951, 39–56. LEWIN, K., LIPPITT, R., and WHITE, R. K., 'Patterns of Aggressive Behaviour in experimentally created "social climates",' *J. Soc. Psychol.*, **10**, 1939, 271–99. These articles discuss the efficiency of learning in different 'social climates' and the ways in which they determine the nature and quality of interactions between members of a group.
4. DEUTSCH, MORTON. 'An Experimental Study of the Effects of Co-operation and Competition upon Group Process.' *Hum. Rel.* **2**, 1949, 199–231.
5. For a fuller discussion of the relation between classroom experience and the development of social maturity see OESER, O. A., 'Training for Democracy: the Use of Group Incentives in the Classroom', in: BEST, R. J. (Ed.), *Education for International Understanding* (Adelaide, New Education Fellowship, 1948). 344–50.
6. RIESMAN, DAVID, *The Lonely Crowd* (London, Geoffrey Cumberlege, 1950; New Haven, Yale University Press).

V

Sociometry

A. P. WARD

Synopsis

THIS chapter is concerned with the problem of the relationships which exist among children in a class. It has three purposes:
(a) to describe simple techniques by which the teacher can obtain a clear picture of the pattern of relationships which exist among the children of his grade;

(b) to give examples from the findings of various researches and actual classroom situations which will help the teacher to interpret the data he obtains;

(c) to show how these techniques can be put to practical use in the classroom.

These techniques are fundamental aids to helping the child to 'want' to learn (that is, 'motivating' the child).

Citizenship is a pattern of social interactions and, like any pattern, can be adequate or inadequate, harmonious or discordant. Since schools exist to teach social skills, the skill of citizenship should also be taught; and, like all skills, it can be learned only through practice. Social studies (or civics) and history can provide a rich intellectual content; but in themselves they do not teach a person how to create and maintain social relations with his fellows.

The skill of rubbing shoulders companionably can be exercised all the time at school. Yet, curiously, teachers spend much time and energy in preventing children from being companionable. Often, for instance, giving and taking are called cheating, or cribbing, or usurping the prerogatives of the teacher and flouting his authority.

This chapter and the next show how the teacher can create the conditions for the practice of good citizenship in the classroom. They also show that the effects of creating these conditions can do astonishing things to the process of learning abstract intellectual material. These chapters follow naturally after the chapters on motivation and on the role of the teacher, since both motivation and the role of the teacher are the products of social forces and social interaction.

Some Simple Examples

At a pre-school centre an observer was gazing through a one-way screen at a group of twenty children, aged four to five years, who were engaged in undirected play activities. In the centre of the room three boys and a girl were co-operating to build a high tower of blocks. On a platform fitted up as a kitchenette with table and chairs, dresser and chinaware, two girls were playing at 'afternoon tea'. Nearby a little girl stood alone, watching their play, but making no attempt to join in. In a corner a boy played alone, building with deep concentration, a flat structure of building blocks. Three boys sitting at a table were playing with dominoes.

Here, at an early stage, were patterns of common human interrelations.

A teacher stood at the window of his classroom watching the children at play in the school-ground. A few of the pupils of his grade, the fifth, were playing with children from lower or higher grades, but their play contacts were confined mostly to their own group.

He noticed that Tom had his usual coterie of four with him. The five boys were all talking at once, but if the teacher knew anything, Tom was talking the loudest and would eventually have his way. A little farther off Bill and Fred were wrestling on the ground like playful puppies. The girls were playing separately from the boys, but Ted, who did not seem to join in the games with his own sex, was hovering around a group of girls, teasing and annoying them.

There was Gwen, standing alone by the school door. She was gazing, wistfully he thought, at three girls playing nearby, but they took no notice of her, and she made no move towards them. 'What a quiet, shy child she is!' he thought. 'Never any trouble in school. Never has to be spoken to. If only I had a class full of children of her type!'

The function of the school as a training ground for the development of techniques of personal interaction should be recognized and used by all teachers. For true mental health, every child, and adult too, must experience the satisfaction and feeling of security which spring from a sense of 'belonging', and from close personal relationships with members of a peer group.

Sociometry is a method of mapping existent interpersonal relationships and can aid the teacher to see them clearly and use them for constructive educational ends. One of its most valuable contributions is Moreno's sociometric test which he defines as 'a technique which consists in an individual choosing his associates for any group of which he is or might become a member' (1).

GROUP STRUCTURE

The sociometric test reveals the feeling which individuals have towards each other *as members of a group*. This feeling, the sociometric term for which is 'tele', may be one of attraction (positive tele) or repulsion (negative tele), or there may be merely indifference.

When children are asked to name those whom they would like in their group for a specific purpose; for example, to work with, to sit near, to play with, and also those whom they would not like to be associated with, the following categories are usually found:

(a) stars—those chosen by a number of individuals;

(b) mutual pairs—where two individuals choose each other in their first two or three choices;

(c) cliques—where three, four or more individuals include each other in their choices;

(d) chains—where A chooses B, B chooses C, C chooses D. etc.

(e) isolates—those whom nobody chooses;

(f) rejectees—those with whom other individuals express a wish *not* to be associated.

Teachers usually know who are the most popular children, the close friends, the isolates, the group that clings to a leader; but these are surface judgments and are accurate only with regard to the more obvious relationships, that is, those explicitly permitted in the school. Observation alone fails to reveal fully the organization of the group.

The sociometric test is very easy to administer, and although the treatment of the data may require a little patience, the resulting picture of the social structure of the grade will be ample reward for the trouble involved. Mary L. Northway says of this test: 'We now possess an instrument as simple to use and as keen in its application as the Binet tests' (2).

Specific Situations; How to administer the tests

Moreno maintains that in order to get reliable and valid data from the test, it is necessary to promise the group that their choices will really be used. For example, if children are asked to write down the names of those next to whom they would like to sit, they should also be told that in the near future the seating arrangements will be altered to conform to their choices.

Some investigators do not feel that the promise of action is necessary and their test takes a form similar to the following:

'Who are your best friends in this group, people you like to run around with? Name one, two or three, or more, or don't name any, as you wish.'

'We don't all like the same people. Name one, two, three, or more in this group whom you definitely do not like.'

Moreno, however, insists that such a test cannot, strictly speaking, be called sociometric. Asking an individual who is his best friend is vague and loosely defined. But if he is asked with whom he would like to sit or work, he is confronted with a concrete situation for which he has to make a decision. Only then does one tap the real structures in which members of a group are contained and which they themselves maintain (3).

The sociometric technique is a 'test' only from the point of view of the experimenter. From the subject's viewpoint it is a means of doing something to arrange his own social environment, so that he can function more adequately in relation to other individuals. It appears, therefore, that the criteria for choice should be specific, and should have immediate interest.

A. P. Ward

The specific situations for which choices are made include:

selecting a companion to sit with;
selecting the ones preferred as friends to go home with after school;
choosing those preferred as work-mates;
choosing companions to have lunch with or play with in the school-ground.

Investigators have found that all the information usually required concerning group structure in a class can be obtained by presenting not more than three or four such situations.

It is often stated in the sociometric literature that the individual's role may alter from situation to situation, and that a child may be an isolate in the classroom but not in the playground or some other situation. This, however, is unusual, as attitudes tend to be generalized to all school situations, and often even beyond these.

Surveys in Victoria have shown repeatedly that an individual who is isolated or rejected in school is likely to receive very few acceptances, or to be actively rejected by group members in other situations as well.

Collecting all Available Data

(a) *Number of situations:* Three, or at most four, criteria will give all the necessary information commonly required, though one situation is usually adequate for purposes of grouping.

(b) *Reasons:* Much illuminating information is obtained if the children are asked to state their reasons for choosing or rejecting individuals. But it is wise not to ask for reasons until the lists of names have been completed. Otherwise, if the children know they have to give reasons, their spontaneous judgments may be suppressed.

(c) *Number of Choices:* Various investigators follow different practices with regard to the number of choices allowed. Some ask the children to write down the name of only one individual as their choice, others specify two, three, or more choices, others allow the children as many choices as they desire.

In a recent investigation in Melbourne it was found that the method of allowing unlimited choices yielded the highest correlation with the laborious method of pair-by-pair comparison, which requires the subjects to make a choice between each pair of individuals in the class in turn, until every child had been compared with every other child.

In any case, it is evident that valuable information is lost if children are not allowed to make as many, or as few, choices as they wish. It is important to know, for example, to what extent an isolate reaches out in all directions in an endeavour to find acceptance somewhere, or whether his isolation has caused him to withdraw from all efforts to make social contacts.

Methods of giving the Test

Method A. Each child is handed a slip of blank paper and told to write his own name at the top. Some experimenters prefer to have the names of all children in the grade written on the blackboard. It is always advisable to write up the names of any children who are absent.

In the sociometric study previously mentioned, the following instructions were used:

(1) 'At the top of a piece of paper in front of you write your name and rule a line under it.'

(2) 'Now that we have decided on a topic of our project, you are to be allowed to work in groups, and these groups will be made up according to your own choices. I'll tell you to-morrow who are in the different groups and you may begin working in them straight away. On the left hand side of your sheet write the name of the person with whom you would most like to work in a group. Underneath write the name of the one you would like next best, then the next, and so on. You may write as many names as you wish, or none at all. Look around and make up your mind, but don't speak to anyone, and don't let anyone know whom you are going to choose.'

(3) 'Now turn over the sheet. This time I want you to write, down the left-hand side of the page, the names of any children with whom you really would *not* like to work in a group. You may write as many names as you like, or none at all. What you write will be known only to myself.'

(Demonstrate on blackboard.)

(4) 'Now, turn back to the first page and beside each name say

why you would like to have that person for a work-mate, then turn over to the second page and say why you would not like to have that person in your group. Remember that I am the only one who will know what you say.'

(A very much more satisfactory, but more time-consuming, method of dealing with Step 4 is to ask each child individually his reasons for choices and rejections.)

Method B. The paper may be divided into compartments, the number depending upon the number of specific situations for which the children have to make choices.

Figure 1 shows a sheet of paper which provides for three criteria—'To work with in a group', 'To sit with', and 'To play with in the schoolground'.

FIGURE 1

Work with YES	*Work with* NO
Sit with YES	*Sit with* NO
Play with YES	*Play with* NO

The children are asked to write their choices, in order of preference, in the boxes marked 'Yes' for each criterion, and in the boxes marked 'No' they write the names of those with whom they would not like to be associated in each situation. It should be pointed out repeatedly that the same child, or children, may be named in more than one category.

METHODS OF PRESENTING THE DATA

There are several ways of depicting the data obtained from a sociometric test. Each has its advantages and disadvantages.

Raw Data

Figure 2 shows a convenient method by which raw data may be recorded when the group is not large. (See 'Notes', below.)

70

Sociometry

FIGURE 2

	A	B	C	D	E	F	G	H
A		+ 3	+ 2	— 1	+ 1	— 2		
B	+ 2		+ 3		+ 1	— 1		— 2
C	+ 3	+ 2			+ 4	+ 1		
D	— 1	+ 1				+ 2	+ 3	— 2
E	+ 2	+ 3	+ 1					
F				+ 1	+ 3		+ 2	— 1
G				+ 1	+ 2	+ 3		
H	+ 4	+ 5	+ 3	+ 1	+ 2			

Names of all children are written vertically down the left-hand side of the chart, and in the same order horizontally along the top. Boys' names are put first, then the girls' names, providing there are few or no cross-sex choices. Where the row containing a child's name intersects with the column containing his name, a cross is put.

Each time a child makes a choice a plus sign is put in his row in the column under the name of the individual he chooses. The figure indicates the order of preference. A minus sign indicates rejection. Thus A chose E, C, and B in that order, and rejected D and F in that order.

(a) The Sociomatrix

The first problem is to decide how many choices to take into consideration when constructing the matrix. All choices and rejections may be shown, in which case it is advisable to show also the figures indicating the order of preference or rejection. On the other hand, it may be decided that, in order to make the data comparable for all subjects, the same number of choices will be shown for each, say, the first two, or else the criterion may be the number of acceptances of the person who made the fewest choices. For example, in Figure 2 the lowest number of choices made by any person is three, so only the first three choices of each individual need to be taken into account when constructing the matrix.

Figure 3 represents a sociomatrix which consists of a rearrangement of the data given in Figure 2. The first three choices only are shown.

Procedure

(1) Construct a blank matrix having as many rows and columns as there are children.

71

(2) Find the individual who received the highest number of first, second and third choices. This is E. Write his name at the side of the first row and at the top of the first column.

(3) Select E's mutual choices.

This may be done by looking down E's column (to see by whom he was chosen) and across his row (to see whom he chose).

Thus he made mutual choices with A, B, and C.

(4) Show these names in the matrix, putting C first as this was a mutual first choice. Plus signs indicate choices as on the raw data sheet.

(5) Mutual choices of C, A, and B are now indicated. If this involved any additional names these would be written on the matrix.

(6) Any unreciprocated choices within the group already represented are recorded.

(7) Rejections within this group are also shown, using minus signs.

(8) Find the individual, not already represented, who is next most highly chosen. This is D. Find his reciprocated choices and proceed as in Steps 3 to 7.

(9) Continue in this way until all names have been dealt with.

Notes

(a) It is advisable to tick off the squares on the raw data chart as each choice or rejection is recorded on the matrix.

(b) When the group is large, the experimenter may find it convenient to dispense with a raw data chart. Instead he may make rough lists of reciprocated choices, and from these construct his sociomatrix.

An examination of Figure 3 will reveal that there are two cliques— E, C, A, B, and D, F, G, while H is an isolate and is also rejected by three people.

It is claimed by those who favour this method (**4**) of presenting sociometric data that the sociogram (see next section) is apt to be confusing, especially if the number of subjects is large.

For some purposes it may be desirable to express all the data available on the sociomatrix, by showing all choices and rejections instead of limiting them to the first three as explained above. Also,

Sociometry

figures showing the order of preference and rejection may be shown in the square.

FIGURE 3

Sociomatrix depicting rearrangement of data shown in Figure 2

	E	C	A	B	D	F	G	H
E		+	+	+				
C	+		+	+				
A	+	+		+	—	—		
B	+	+	+			—		—
D			—	+		+	+	—
F	+				+		×	—
G	+				+	+		
H	+	+			+			

(b) *The Sociogram*

The sociogram is the original method of presenting the data, and is still a very popular method. Each individual may be represented by a circle with his name or initials in it; or if there are both sexes they may be represented by different symbols.

There are different ways of showing the *tele* which exists between two individuals. One way is to show attraction by a broken line and rejection by an unbroken line. Arrow heads are used to show the direction of the *tele*.

Thus, if A accepts B and C, if B accepts A but rejects C, and if C rejects both A and B, the situation would be represented as in Figure 4.

FIGURE 4

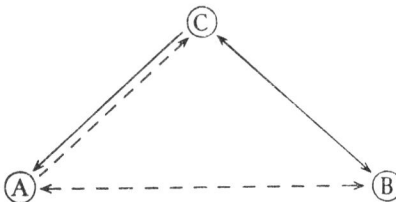

A. P. Ward

The data shown in the sociomatrix (Figure 3) have been rearranged in sociogram form in Figure 5.

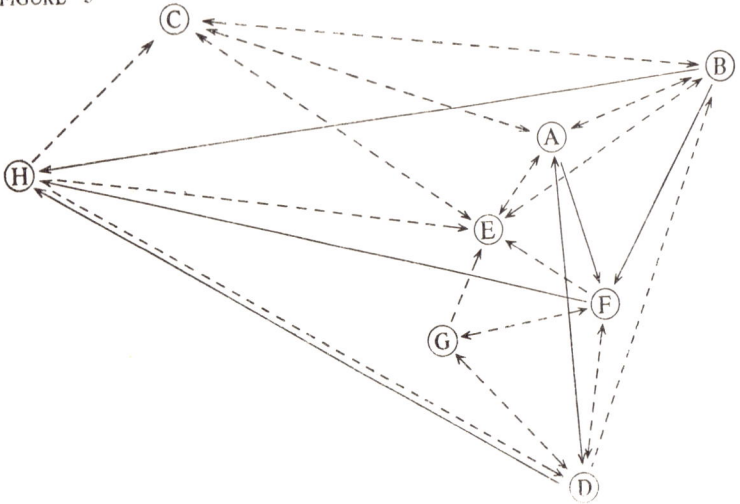

FIGURE 5

According to Moreno (5) the value of this method of presentation lies in the fact that complex relationships such as triangles, chains, and stars are directly visible. Also, when an individual rejects, and is in conflict with the key individual of an important sub-group, the situation may be clearly depicted. Note, in Figure 5, the clearly represented triangle composed of the individuals D, F, G; the clique A, B, C, E; the star E, and the isolate H who is also rejected by D, F, and B.

If the relationships of a large group are being depicted in a sociogram, the picture will be confusing if too many data are included. Many experimenters, therefore, show acceptances on one sociogram and rejections on another. Again, if both sexes are represented in the group and there are no cross-sex choices, girls and boys may be shown on separate charts.

Sociometry

Overlapping Groups

When a matrix or sociogram is being constructed from the group data, it is usual to find that grouping is not simple and clear-cut. Quite often one finds distinct groups which have certain members common to both groups. On the sociomatrix this situation shows up clearly as one of the overlapping groups. If there are no inter-group rejections the two groups may work together harmoniously. Sometimes the key position in both groups is held by one individual; but when leadership is divided, an attempt to bring the two groups together for some co-operative project might result in friction.

Sub-groups within Groups

The sociometric picture is often complicated by groups having within them sub-groups, as shown in Figure 6.

FIGURE 6

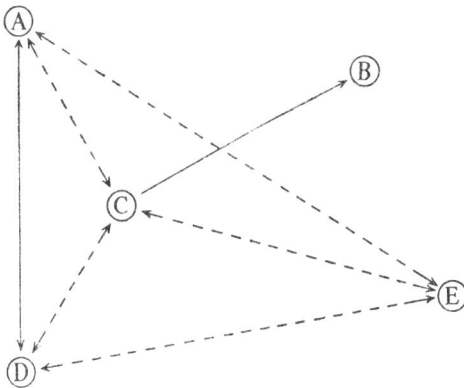

In this group of five individuals there are two definite triangles —C,E,D, and C,E,A. It will be seen that C and E are members of both sub-groups, but A and D mutually reject each other. A situation such as this would lead to an interesting exercise in observation to see how these relationships affected each other. Much might depend on the attitude of C and the relative strength of his acceptances of A and D.

75

Other sub-groupings which do not involve rejections are B,D,E, and A,B,E.

Choices outside the Group

It is sound practice, when giving the sociometric test, to allow the children to make choices from other classes if they so desire. This may provide a measure of how well integrated the class is. For example, in a poorly integrated class there may be many choices outside the group. Also, new light may be thrown on the position of certain individuals. For example, John was an isolate, or near isolate, within the class, but his first choices went outside the group. This could have indicated that he had quite satisfactory social relationships, and was not disturbed by his lack of acceptance in the class; or it might have indicated a desire to escape from that class.

SOCIAL RELATIONSHIPS AMONG NURSERY SCHOOL CHILDREN

The social relationships of children at this stage, 3 to 5 years, may be studied by direct observation and by sociometric methods.

At the age of three years children are just beginning to play in a co-operative manner and to develop preferences, and it is not until the later pre-school stage that significant social relationships are formed. The sociometric methods, therefore, are more suited to the older nursery school children.

The direct observation of behaviour may be more reliably carried out by using the technique known as 'time-sampling'. It should be noted that observation cannot be used as a substitute for sociometric techniques. The two methods are complementary.

The use of sociometric methods with young children presents several problems.

(a) *Verbal expression of preferences.* Pre-school children do have preferences. Investigators differ, however, as to the significance of the levels of preference. Some believe that with young children only the first choice matters, and the other preferences may be determined by observation. Others consider that the pre-school child can express a number of choices verbally, but his levels of preference are best determined by the frequency with which he names the children.

Sociometry

(b) *Meaningfulness of test questions.* Meaningfulness is best attained when the results of the test can be put into immediate operation. Preschool children find it easier to make choices for a natural, familiar situation than for hypothetical situations which are not related to the immediate setting. Moreno, for example, used the following formula:

'You are going to play with blocks now. Whom would you like to come and play with you?'

(c) *Administration of the test.* E. B. Frankel (6) describes a test involving situations which have meaning for the child. Before the test is given the child is shown a picture book, and the contents are discussed to counteract the influence of any social contacts immediately preceding the test. This also helps to establish rapport. Then the tester asks the following questions:

(1) What do you like playing with in the garden? Whom do you like to play that with best? Whom else? Whom else?
(2) What do you like doing in the playroom? Whom do you like to play that with best? Whom else? Whom else?
(3) And now tell me whom do you like to sit with best when you eat lunch? Whom else? Whom else?

In addition to this test time-sampling methods of observation are used to note the children's contacts during the free play period in the playground of the nursery school. It is thus possible to compare their preferences as expressed verbally and their actual playmates in the play situation.

Time-sampling and sociometric methods do not measure quite the same things. Because of this discrepancy it is advisable to use both methods in studying the social relationships of nursery school children. Or, if strict time-sampling be not used, careful observations should at least be made to supplement the sociometric data.

Ken said he liked to play with Laurie, Ernie, and Alan, but in the playground during the period of observation he played only with Laurie. Although verbal choices and actual contacts are not always identical, there are some interesting relationships. For example, children who receive a large number of verbal preferences usually have many contacts in the playground. Most of the children in the group said they would like to play with Alan, and in the playground he received the highest score for the number of different contacts made.

The relationships between a child's verbal choices and his actual contacts may indicate the necessity for guidance and therapy. Tony said he liked to play with Alan, Harry, and Charlie. He also volunteered the information that he liked to play with Laurie, Ernie and Donald. In the playground he was observed to approach Ernie, but was rebuffed. After this he made no further attempt to play with anyone, but simply watched other children playing. It is significant that Tony named six children with whom he liked to play, but that no one named him or made contact with him in the play situation. He was an isolate in both cases.

APPLICATIONS OF SOCIOMETRY

Sociometric methods have been successfully used in schools, factories, prisons, orphanages, homes for delinquents, and mental hospitals. Almost any issue of the Journal *Sociometry* contains accounts of the use of these techniques in various situations, but here the discussion will be limited to education.

(a) *Advantages of a Knowledge of Social Status*

The Leader. Bernice, in the teacher's opinion, was a dependable child with a strong character. Would she make a good form captain? Ordinary voting methods would reveal how far she was accepted, but would not show the extent of feeling against her. The sociometric data indicated that she was a very popular girl, and that she was not rejected by anyone. One other girl received as high an acceptance score, but at the same time was actively rejected by a number of children.

The Quiet Child. Nina was a quiet, shy child. She was not chosen by anyone, and was rejected by several. She was placed in a group of well-adjusted children, none of whom had rejected her. For further information concerning this case the reader is referred to Chapter 5.

The Young Delinquent. Norman was a black sheep of the class. He had had two brushes with the police, and was always in trouble with members of staff at the school. He was not a complete isolate, but was rejected by a number of children. Some of the reasons given for rejecting him were illuminating: 'He tells lies', 'He gets you into trouble', 'He is a thief', 'He cheats', 'He is dirty'.

Norman's case is interesting and is discussed more fully in Chapter 6. The social relationships of the delinquent or the socially malad-justed child with other members of the group provide valuable in-formation, and a better understanding of his problems can be had by knowing the relations between his school situation and his home environment.

(b) *The Introduction of Group Methods of Teaching*

The sociometric test provides the teacher with data which can be used to organize the class into groups composed of individuals who have expressed feelings of attraction for one another.

The application of group methods and specific problems concerned with the introduction of these methods are discussed in Chapter 6.

(c) *The Development of Social Relations*

Studies of groups of babies (1) show that the individuals go through the stages of complete isolation, reaction to immediate neighbours, then differentiation with regard to the amount of attention they command. In the nursery school years they develop social status—that is, some are chosen more often and have more playmates than others. This stage is of great importance as a basis for social and personality development.

The percentage of isolation in the nursery, first and second grades, is higher than in any of the subsequent stages, and the number of mutual choices is lower. Children in these grades are not yet certain whom to choose. The high proportion of isolates found in the 4–7 age group does not appear to be due to the fact that these children are disliked or actively rejected. They are simply left out. At later stages children are isolated not only because they are forgotten, or left out, but because others in the group have formed definite attitudes towards them. The gradual development of attitudes towards each other as children grow older no doubt helps to explain why fewer cases of isolation and a greater number of mutual choices are found in the higher grades. Also, the cliques, triangles, and chains found among older children are absent in the nursery and first grades.

Children at the kindergarten and first grade level tend to make

A. P. Ward

choices irrespective of sex, but after this stage there is a sudden drop in cross-sex choices, and it is then rare, in Victorian State schools, to find boys choosing girls, or girls choosing boys. Even at the adolescent stage cultural taboos tend to keep choices to one sex group

(d) *Contributions of Sociometry to the Study of Personality*

Sociometry, being concerned with the relationships which exist between people, has made a number of contributions to our under-standing of personality characteristics associated with friendship, social status, leadership and adolescence.

(i) *Friendship.* What are the factors which cause two people to be mutually attracted? M. E. Bonney (7) found some evidence to indicate that children who form friendships are likely to be approximately equal in academic achievement and in general intelligence and to have very similar home backgrounds. It was concluded that the socio-economic and cultural level of a child's home plays a small part in determining the friendships he forms.

R. Potashin (8) found that objective, measurable, factors such as height, weight, chronological age, mental age, intelligence quotient, academic achievement, and parents' occupational status and residence, may act as limiting factors. For example, the fact that Tom, Bill, Fred, and John live in the same neighbourhood, or are alike in certain characteristics, increases the likelihood of friendships being formed, but does not explain why Tom chooses Fred as a friend rather than Bill or John.

Potashin also made a comparative study of pairs of children. When two friends were together they stayed longer, talked more freely, and were more relaxed. When poorly accepted children were with non-friends they brought tension into the situation. The behaviour of these children was often annoying to the partner. They either tended to watch the other for cues and agree with everything he said, or else they tried to make an impression by talking a great deal, showing off, and approving enthusiastically of all the partner's ideas.

By using a scale designed to measure the capacity to win friends, Bonney (7) found that the following traits were important:

Praising and complimenting others; initiating discussions about topics of general interest and about the particular interests of individuals; tolerance and adaptability; group association and group

80

participation; stimulating people to higher levels of behaviour; dependence on others for assistance and emotional support; dependability; being a source of new experience to others; emotional control; helpfulness and social service motivation; health and physical vigour; personal appearance; abiding by group customs and morals; attitude towards one's self.

(ii) *Isolation and Low Status.* Case studies of isolated children show that they are likely to be either recessive or aggressive. The recessive, that is, the shy, withdrawn type of child, seems to lack energy and enthusiasm. Bonney (9) suggests that when moral or religious education overemphasizes docility, submission to authority and conformity, this may seriously affect the child's social acceptability. The aggressive isolate indulges in such forms of behaviour as destructiveness, interference with others, boisterousness, and rudeness.

The extent of a child's acceptability to others seems to be related to the amount and the direction of 'outgoing energy' he displays. The child who shows little energy, the recessive isolate, is *not accepted*; the child whose energy results in interference with the activity of others, the aggressive isolate, is *rejected*. Isolates appear to be self-interested, and show little ability to appreciate the thoughts and feelings of others.

(iii) *Leadership.* Sociometric studies show that leadership cannot be explained simply by reference to the possession of certain personality traits. It depends, rather, on the contribution which the individual can make in a specific situation. The leader helps others towards goals which they desire to reach. The 'star', or most widely accepted person, is not always the leader. The real leader may be one who has close connections with the star, and through him is able to lead the group.

Jennings (10) states that 'leaders are persons who exert exceptional efforts on behalf of other members, in a manner which the latter recognize as constructive and representing their interests'.

(iv) *Adolescence.* At no stage in school life can sociometric techniques be used to better advantage than at the secondary level, for with the heightened sensibility characteristic of adolescence, social isolation or rejection may cause the individual acute suffering.

Parents, counsellors, and teachers, when considering individual cases of adjustment, the dislike of school and the desire to leave, must take into account the possibility that the child is attempting to escape from an intolerable social situation.

Research (11) into this problem has shown that children of low sociometric status, that is, those who receive few or no acceptances, usually experience feelings of social insecurity and unhappiness. They *feel* isolated, and are conscious of a lack of social skills. These children also experience family difficulties more often than do well-accepted children.

These difficulties include unsuitable clothes, poor economic circumstances, and low cultural standards of the parents or tension between them. Sociometric surveys in Victoria, however, have shown that in the formation of the attitudes of children to an individual, it is their *subjective* estimates of various attributes which are of importance rather than objective factors, such as socio-economic class or intelligence quotient. That is, if the children *perceive* an individual as having undesirable attributes, he may be rejected or ignored regardless of class, intelligence, and other measurable characteristics.

Adjustment at home and at school are highly correlated. Children who, at home, are over-protected or rejected, mother-dominated or over-indulged, figure largely in the ranks of the socially maladjusted at school. Broken homes, quarrels, and parental infantilism also contribute.

The teacher's concern is with what can be done in the school to improve the status of these children. Very often a tactful approach to parents will remove some of the more obvious handicaps, such as poor clothing and lack of cleanliness. But the school must have a positive programme for training social skills. Just as one method of overcoming fear is to teach skills which aid in coping with fear-arousing situations, so children may be trained to overcome social handicaps by teaching them skills such as making introductions, dancing, posture, correct clothing and personal hygiene.

Conclusions. The sociometric test taps outcomes of education which cannot be measured by the ordinary examination methods. Apart from its use for grouping purposes, the test is valuable in detecting signs of social ill-health and in gauging the effectiveness of therapeutic measures.

Sociometry

The frustrations to which children are so often subjected in their home and neighbourhood environment and which are frequently aggravated by the classroom situation, often result in aggression which reveals itself in a large number of active rejections, the formation of tight in-groups or cliques whose members have little or no inter-communication with others, in scapegoating, and in the isolation of some children.

The teacher who decides to do something about the social relationships of his pupils, and embarks upon a programme of education based on the principles set forth in this book, has, in the sociometric test, a means of measuring objectively any changes which may result in the relationships of the children.

A sociometric test administered after the programme has been given an adequate trial should provide interesting comparisons with a test given at the beginning. Signs of better social health would include the disappearance of isolates and a decrease in the number of rejections, less confinement of choices within cliques, and the appearance of cross-sex choices.

A problem which arises in some classrooms is that of race discrimination and prejudice. In schools in which there is a large immigrant element this situation should be carefully watched. The existence of prejudice can be quickly detected on a sociogram, and steps taken to circumvent it. Changes in attitudes can be measured by subsequent tests.

This chapter has been concerned with sociometric tests and group structure. In the following chapter the application of sociometric data to the formation of groups for group methods of teaching is discussed, and some of the cases and problems raised in this chapter are amplified.

SELECTED REFERENCES FOR FURTHER READING

1. MORENO, J. L., *Who Shall Survive* (Washington, Nervous and Mental Disease Publishing Company, 1934). In this book Moreno sets out a technique of group analysis, the data for this analysis being derived from a sociometric test. According to Moreno a sociometric test 'consists in an individual choosing his associates for any group of which he is, or might become a member'. The author maintains that the promise of action to result from the choices is the required motivating force which will ensure reliable and valid responses.

A. P. Ward

2. NORTHWAY, MARY L., 'Sociometry and Some Challenging Problems of Social Relationships', *Sociometry*, **9**, No. 3, 1946. Four problems are discussed. These are stated as hypotheses, or formulations set up for the purpose of being investigated. The hypotheses are:

(i) 'An individual's acceptance score as measured in one group is a reliable index to what his acceptance will be in a reasonably similar (cultural-age) group. That is, his acceptance score is an outward measure of a psychological characteristic called acceptability.'

(ii) 'Anything which served to unite the members of a group to the achievement of a common cause and provided opportunity for co-operative participation would increase the measurable cohesiveness of that group. . . . As competition and individual success were emphasized within the group cohesiveness would measurably decrease.'

(iii) 'Scientific studies using sociometric techniques could be designed not only to discover preferences but to ascertain the relationship of prejudice to these.'

(iv) 'Investigations could be set up to demonstrate individual differences in form of response to failure situations.'

3. MORENO, J. L., 'Progress and Pitfalls in Sociometric Theory', *Sociometry*, **10**, No. 3, 1947. The author discusses the difficulty of the definition and analysis of social criteria used in administering the sociometric test. The more specific the criteria the better are the chances of tapping the real structure of a group. He warns against a tendency to use interviews and observational techniques to supplant the sociometric test. The hypothesis is discussed that 'a cleavage exists between private and social within every individual and in every group'.

4. FORSYTH, E., and KATZ, L., 'A Matrix Approach to the Analysis of Sociometric Data', *Sociometry*, **9**, No. 4, 1946. The difficulties and deficiencies of presenting the data obtained from a sociometric test in 'sociogram' form are pointed out, and a method of preserving all the data by using a 'sociomatrix' is described.

5. MORENO, J. L., 'Sociogram and Sociomatrix,' *Sociometry*, **9**, No. 4, 1946. Moreno replies to the statements made by Forsyth and Katz concerning the superiority of the sociomatrix over the sociogram. He claims that in depicting certain group structures, such as triangles and chain relations, the sociogram is superior. It is recognized, however, that each method has advantages and may be used to supplement the other.

6. FRANKEL, ESTHER B., 'The Social Relationships of Nursery School Children', *Sociometry*, **9**, No. 3, 1946. This paper is based on research conducted for the purpose of studying the social relationships of nursery school children. There is a comparison of methods for studying social relationships—the sociometric test and observation of play contacts. The two methods measure supplementary aspects of social

84

relationships. There is also a discussion of factors related to social relationships under the headings:

(*a*) Objective factors, such as age and length of time of membership in a group.

(*b*) The child's social relationships and his social scores.

(*c*) Emotional and non-conformity behaviour.

It was found that objective factors have little or no correlation with children's social scores, and the most fruitful approach for obtaining clues in the area of interpersonal relationships is by studying the personality development of the child.

7. BONNEY, M. E., 'A Sociometric Study of the Relationship of Some Factors to Mutual Friendships on the Elementary, Secondary and College Levels', *Sociometry*, 9, No. 1, 1946. This study contributes to the problem of determining the factors which influence the formation of mutual attractions. It throws light on the relationship between mutual friendship formation and academic achievement, intelligence, certain kinds of interests, socio-economic home background and personality traits.

8. POTASHIN, R., 'A Sociometric Study of Children's Friendship'' *Sociometry*, 9, No. 1, 1946. Three aspects of friendship are examined:

(i) Objective characteristics related to friendship.

(ii) The social sphere within which friendship functions.

(iii) The relationship in action within a controlled setting.

The aim of this study is to clarify the relationship of friendship. From it has been obtained 'a feeling of what friendship is like, an indication of the general atmosphere it involves and a little of the relationship between this interaction and the personality make-up of the individual'.

9. BONNEY, M. E., 'Personality Traits of Socially Successful and Socially Unsuccessful Children', *J. Ed. Psych.*, 34, 1943. This study highlights the effects of conditioning—e.g., moral or religious education—on the social acceptability of the child. The child who shows up as an isolate may be either shy and withdrawn, and lacking in energy and enthusiasm, or he may be aggressive, and engage in bullying, destructiveness, etc. The former is the type which is likely to be just not accepted, while the aggressive type is likely to be actively rejected in the group.

10. JENNINGS, H. H., 'Leadership and Sociometric Choice'. In *Readings in Social Psychology*, (Ed.) Newcomb and Hartley. (New York, Holt, 1947). This is an account of an investigation carried out at the New York State Training School for Girls, an institution for girls committed by the Children's Courts of the State. The problem of the report is to note the relation between behaviour shown in interaction with others and the sociometric choice status of the individual. High choice status is found to be closely related to leadership. Leadership appears to be explainable, not by any personality quality or constellation of traits,

but because of 'the interpersonal contribution of which the individual becomes capable in a specific setting eliciting such contributions from him'. An analysis of the ways of behaving of the highly chosen individuals shows that the leadership they exert is definable as 'a manner of interacting with others—a manner which moves others in directions apparently desired by the latter'. 'This is not a generalized capacity which may relate the person to all other individuals. . . . It appears in the special sensitivity between the individual and *specific* other persons, resulting in interaction between them.'

11. KUHLEN, R. G., and BRETSCH, H. S., 'Sociometric Status and Personal Problems of Adolescents', *Sociometry*, **10**, No. 2, 1947. The data reported in this paper were obtained from 692 ninth grade adolescents. Sociometric status of these boys and girls was determined, and evidence was obtained as to the personal problems characterizing them. The general finding was that the unaccepted children had more problems than the more accepted. Difficulties concerned with social skills, unhappiness and lack of status, family problems, and dislike of school, figured prominently among the problems of the least accepted.

VI

Problems and Effects of Changing the
Social Structure of the
Classroom

A. P. WARD and L. J. MURPHY

Synopsis

THE purpose of this chapter is to discuss some of the problems likely to be encountered when group methods are introduced for the first time. It offers advice about criteria for assigning children to groups and deals with the difficulties teachers meet under present conditions in the classroom. Specific suggestions are made about the procedure to be followed in organizing group activities and in the concluding section an attempt is made to deal with the outcomes of group work.

Two cases illustrate the danger of attempting to use group teaching methods without a sound understanding of the techniques and the theory outlined in this and other chapters of the book.

After attending a refresher course, mentioned in the preface, on the social psychology of the classroom, Mr. X returned to his school full of enthusiasm to put into practice group methods of teaching. The result of his experiment was extremely disappointing. Motivation appeared to be lacking, and serious problems of behaviour arose.

A. P. Ward and L. J. Murphy

Two errors contributed to the causes of his failure. Firstly he grouped the children on the single criterion of sociometric choice, and secondly, he put in one group five children, all rejectees, some of whom were chronic behaviour problems.

Mr. Y did not attend the refresher school, but he knew a teacher who had, and from him heard about group methods. Unfortunately, he heard only half the story. He did not understand sociometric choices and group structure, so he assigned the children to groups as they sat, then promptly informed them that this arrangement did not mean that they could regard school as a place where social calls were made.

At the end of a week Mr. Y abandoned the scheme. The children had not done any more work than usual and the method had encouraged copying and talking in class.

The group method is not a panacea which will solve all the problems of the weak or incompetent teacher, the autocratic teacher, or the boring teacher. It is not meant to supplant class teaching, but to supplement and enrich it. Class teaching of a stimulating kind can be a source of inspiration and encouragement, which contributes to the satisfaction of the needs of both child and teacher. (See Chapter 4 on permissive and directive teaching.)

What Subjects are Suitable for Group Methods?

Group methods have been successfully used by the authors in mathematics, English, and social studies. The methods, however, may profitably be applied in all parts of the curriculum, though the proportions of class (or directive) teaching and individual work will vary with the subject.

On what Criteria should Children be Assigned to Groups?

One method is to allow the children to form their own groups. Objections to this method are that the more forceful children may gather their satellites around them and perhaps form unhealthy nuclei in the class; some pupils may find themselves in groups where certain members reject them; and unwanted children will feel left out.

Mr. X, it will be remembered, administered a sociometric test and then assigned his pupils to groups, using only the criterion of

88

sociometric choice. His procedure was especially faulty in this case because the subject for which he tried the group method was arithmetic.

Mr. Y assigned the children to groups as they sat. This teacher believed in seating children in rows according to their ability, so that the best pupils were at one end of the room and the worst pupils at the other. Thus the criterion by which Mr. Y in fact grouped the children was really ability.

As a rule the soundest plan is to group the pupils according to their choices in the sociometric test, but to be guided also by their ability, as revealed by a test, or as judged by the teacher.

The importance of forming groups of children who are not only acceptable to one another, but are fairly evenly matched in academic ability, will be seen if it is understood what happens if bright and dull pupils are put together. Usually the bright ones do the work and the duller ones copy. The latter, therefore, do not develop their own abilities, tend to lose confidence in themselves, and become resentful. The bright children, on the other hand, become resentful because the others are not pulling their weight. But the great value of the group method is the opportunity it provides for the satisfaction of social needs. This satisfaction depends on being accepted by the group, and acceptance is directly related to the contribution that is made to the group effort.

The criteria of sociometric choice and ability apply especially to mathematics and certain branches of English, but ability in mathematics is not necessarily related to ability in English. It may be wise, therefore, to re-group for different subjects if necessary.

In social studies the grouping may be more elastic. In one experiment, for example, it was found that when a class was grouped on the basis of the above criteria, all children in two of the groups could not agree on the choice of a topic. When this happened the children re-grouped on the basis of their interests. (See 'Work Groups and Activity Programmes' in a later section of this chapter.)

How to deal with Special Cases

When groups are being formed, the children who are not chosen by anyone, the isolates, should be given very special consideration. As was mentioned in Chapter 5, isolated children may be quiet, shy, recessive children, or else they may try to make up for their low social status by aggressive behaviour. The child who is not actively rejected may or may not be an isolate, but he, too, needs special attention.

What is important is that these are socially maladjusted children, and a strong justification for using the sociometric test is that it throws their problems into relief, and enables the teacher to take positive steps to help in their social development.

The Isolate. Barbara, a shy, unwanted child, was placed with a group of girls whom the teacher knew to be well adjusted. A few quiet, confidential words with these girls resulted in Barbara being chosen as secretary for the group. Observation of this group revealed that she became an accepted member, and it was pleasing to see the animation and comparative lack of reticence with which she entered into the discussions and activities.

The Rejected Child. Norman lived with an aunt and his mother (a woman of somewhat questionable virtue) in a poor quarter of the town. His uncle used the house as a place to come to each time he was let out of gaol. His father's identity and whereabouts were unknown. Norman had been caught on shop premises and warned by the police. He was a truant, and frequently bullied children from lower grades.

To do much for such a case seems to be beyond the power of the teacher. What was needed was a change of environment, and Norman was heading fast for such a change. In the meantime the teacher had to do the best he could with the means at his disposal. Fortunately, teachers do not have many problems as bad as this, but the way this one was handled is a good illustration of what can be done.

What was to be done with a boy who had been rejected on the grounds that he was dirty, that he got people into trouble, that he told lies, etc.? The teacher did not immediately assign Norman to a group. Instead he asked the lad if he would help in preparing some material for a project, and to look around and see which group he would like to join. When the boy made his choice, the teacher considered the individuals in the group, then decided to take them into his confidence. In the meantime the teacher pointed out to Norman that if he wanted these boys to have him as a mate, he would have to come to school clean and tidy.

90

Problems and Effects of Changing the Social Structure

Later the boys of the selected group were called in and the teacher informed them that Norman had said he wanted to work with them. He told them that he wanted very much to do something to help the boy, and asked them if they could make any suggestions. They themselves said that it would be a good plan to keep this a private matter. At last came the suggestion from the boy who had been chosen as leader that, when Norman entered the group, they should hold another election and choose him as leader. The teacher was staggered at this proposal, and his first impulse was to disagree. But the other boys at once accepted the idea, and with many misgivings he let them have their way.

This is not a fairy story. It does not end with Norman as the best adjusted and most popular boy in the class. What can be said is that for two whole months he came to school washed, his hair combed, and his boots cleaned; that during that time he did not miss one day; and that he took an inordinate pride in the achievements of the group.

Norman is now in a home for delinquent boys. The effects of his home environment were too powerful, and he broke into a shop once too often. But for a short time, at least his school environment had been made a little more pleasant, and the boys of the group had a worth-while experience in social work.

General Remarks concerning the Treatment of the Socially Maladjusted. As a rule, isolates and rejectees should be set to work with well-accepted children who have not rejected them, and among whom are some chosen by these maladjusted children. The social acceptability of these children can be improved by giving them responsibilities that will make them of use to others. The teacher can arrange that they be put into positions where they will be noticed, and brought into contact with other members of the class—for example, giving out library books, keeping records, acting as chairman or secretary of a committee; *but he must do this without using autocratic methods.*

The Placement of Friends. Should friends be allowed to sit together? Yes; but teachers often separate friends on the grounds that they talk and do not get their work done. When this is the case, the teacher can be reasonably sure that motivating factors are at fault. It can confidently be asserted that, when grouping based on congenial social relationships is given a fair trial, and the criteria for satisfactory motivation are met, there will be a marked improvement in attitudes, behaviour, and scholastic progress.

Problems Arising in 'Platoon Systems'. Objections are sometimes raised that it is difficult to introduce group methods in schools where pupils go from room to room for various subjects, or where they stay in the same room and different teachers take the different subjects, or where one teacher is a pioneer, and the only one on a staff who wishes to try out group methods.

Miss M was in just such a situation. Faced with scepticism on the part of certain members of staff, she resolutely set to work to try out the group method with one form to which she taught arithmetic. Her session with this form followed, and preceded, periods taken by two other teachers, both of whom were authoritarian in their methods, and stern disciplinarians. The teacher who followed Miss M complained that when she came into the room, the children were restless and it took her several minutes to restore them to 'normal'. Miss M's difficulty was that she was trying to introduce democratic procedures immediately after the children had been exposed to authoritarian treatment.

The work of Lewin and his collaborators has important implications for education. In controlled, experimental situations it was found that when children are submitted to changes of 'climate'—that is, from authoritarian to democratic, or from democratic to authoritarian types of classroom management—they frequently react by resorting to anti-social forms of behaviour, such as mischief, aggressiveness, and 'horseplay'.

At first the results of Miss M's experiment were most discouraging. She tried to introduce the method too suddenly and the children tended to take undue advantage of their new freedom. Also, instead of mere scepticism, she now had to face open opposition from at least one member of staff. Miss M, however, was an excellent teacher and very persistent. As the novelty wore off, and the children began to experience the satisfactions of group membership, they gradually came to accept the situation. Their attitudes improved, and the other teacher ceased complaining.

It should be stressed that the weak or inexperienced teacher will not find that, by introducing group work, all his problems of motivation and discipline will disappear. For the method to be successful, the teacher must have the confidence and respect of his pupils. The children must be able to regard the teacher as a friendly person, sincerely interested in them as individuals.

How to form Groups

Use of Criteria. It has already been stated that it is usually advisable to group children on the bases of sociometric choice and ability. But what criterion is to be used for judging ability?

An experienced teacher who knows the children well can usually grade them according to ability fairly accurately, but where this cannot be done, or where more precise methods are required, e.g. for the purpose of controlling groups in an experimental investigation, it is necessary to use an objective measure such as an intelligence test or an achievement test.

Whether an intelligence test or an achievement test is the more appropriate depends on the purpose for which grouping is done. If the class is divided into groups to do arithmetic, then undoubtedly a well-planned arithmetic test is the better criterion, because a child with a high I.Q. does not necessarily excel in that subject.

In order to illustrate how the criteria may be used, an actual example is set out below using data from a mixed class of boys and girls. This was a fifth grade (age about eleven years), and, as is usually the case at this level, no cross-sex choices were made in the sociometric test. The purpose for which the grouping was made was to carry out under controlled experimental conditions an investigation to test the merits of group work methods in arithmetic.

(*a*) The Arithmetic Achievement Tests, Parts 1–6, of the Australian Council for Educational Research were administered to the grade.

(*b*) On the results of these tests the children were classified into three categories—above average, average, and below average.

(*c*) A Sociometric Test was given, the children indicating both their choices and rejections for group work.

(*d*) The slips of paper showing sociometric choices were sorted into three heaps, each individual's slip being put into the category in which he had been classified by (*b*) above.

(*e*) Using the criterion of sociometric choices, and taking care not to put an individual with children who had rejected him, the experimenter assigned the pupils to groups of four within the category in which they had been classified on the basis of arithmetical achievement. The following data indicate how this was done.

Eight boys, A, B, C, D, E, F, G and H were classified as above average. The sociometric data showed that—

A chose B, D, G.	Thus, A was chosen by B, E, F, G, H.
B „ A, G, F.	B „ „ „ A, H.
C „ D, F, H.	C „ „ „ D.
D „ C, H, K.	D „ „ „ A, C, H.
E „ A, G, H.	E „ „ „ none.
F „ A, H, L.	F „ „ „ B, C.
G „ A, M, L.	G „ „ „ A, B, E.
H „ A, B, D.	H „ „ „ C, D, E, F.

A – B and A – G were mutual choices, and B chose G, so that A, B and G could be placed together in a group.

C – H and D – H were mutual choices: F chose H and C chose F. None of these four, C, D, F, and H, was rejected, so they formed a group in which each was chosen by at least one other. E was not chosen by any of the boys in the above average group, but he was placed with A, B, and G, as he was not rejected by any of them and was equal to them in arithmetical achievement. It is of interest to note here that in a later sociometric test, E was chosen by both A and G.

A fairly high degree of correlation will usually be found between academic achievement and sociometric choices. This is especially so where teachers have grouped children in rows according to ability. But instances often occur in which children's choices and acceptances fall outside the academic grouping to which they have been assigned. In such cases the teacher must explain that he has done his best to place all pupils according to their choices, and that where this has not been possible he has placed individuals in groups where they will be able to help other members.

The Problem of Freedom. A class which has been used to autocratic control may, if given too much freedom too suddenly, indulge in anti-social behaviour, because the pupils have not been trained to use freedom properly. Children must be carefully *trained* to work in groups. The reason why some teachers become discouraged when they adopt group methods is that they suddenly plunge a class into the new situation, and expect the children to be able to cope with entirely novel conditions and responsibilities.

On the first day it may be wise to give the groups one specific, simple task which can be successfully completed in five to ten minutes. This should be followed by a class discussion in which the children are invited to express their opinions concerning the merits of group work, and they may be asked for suggestions for making the method successful. A number of quite short sessions will probably be necessary, followed by discussions as to what went wrong, and how the method could be improved. The time allowed for group work and the scope of the assignments or goals can be gradually increased as the children show their readiness.

PROBLEMS CONNECTED WITH THE PHYSICAL SET-UP OF CLASSROOMS

Seating. The desks at present so widely used are heavy and clumsy. The teacher who wishes to introduce group and activity methods is therefore faced with the problem of how to arrange the furniture so that the children can work together in groups of four, five or six.

Re-arrangement of Desks. This is most practical where one teacher has the grade throughout the day. Some teachers, having dual desks to cope with, place pairs of desks facing each other, so that the children can work in fours. The disadvantage of this is that when a class lesson is given, the desks have to be shifted or else the children have to strain round to face the teacher.

Another method is to place pairs of desks wedgewise, or in V formation, with all desks facing towards the board. The desks, of course, will not be parallel to the board, but the children can see it without undue strain.

Leaving Desks in Rows. For various reasons it is not always practicable to re-arrange the desks. When teachers or pupils go from room to room for different subjects, too much time may be lost during the change-over, and in addition, the noise of shifting heavy furniture may disturb other grades. Some head teachers forbid the shifting of desks.

95

This need not deter the teacher from introducing group work. The method has been successfully used with the desks left in the orthodox rows and having the children work in groups of four. When necessary the two front children of a group can swing round and sit facing the other two. This is far from being an ideal arrangement, but it does at least make group work possible.

Lighting. Even more vexatious than the seating is the lighting of most existing schools. Lighting engineers say that the minimum illumination needed for reading is 15 foot-candles—a foot-candle being the amount of light that falls on a surface one foot away from a candle. A very small percentage of schoolrooms has even these minimum requirements uniformly throughout the room. Most rooms have windows along one wall, and illumination varies from 100 foot-candles near the windows to sometimes less than 5 foot-candles on the other side of the room. The usual safeguards about glare, light coming from the left, light paint, etc., should, of course, be observed.

Work Groups and Activity Programmes

The sociometric study mentioned in the preceding chapter was carried out in connection with a project which involved three grades of primary school children—a sixth grade of boys, a sixth grade of girls, and a fifth grade of boys and girls. The procedure was as follows:

(*a*) The children were given a questionnaire on radio programmes. This was followed by a class discussion, which stimulated so much interest that it was decided to carry out a project connected with the topic of 'radio'.

(*b*) Pupils suggested topics which could be investigated and activities which could be carried out. The list included:

The history of radio.
Geography—location of radio stations, raw materials and their sources.
Preparing a script for a radio play.
Making crystal sets.
Finding out how sound travels.
Art—designs for cabinets, illustrations for charts.

(*c*) A sociometric test was given and the children were told that next day they would be assigned to groups on the basis of their choices.

(*d*) They copied out the list of suggested topics, and were asked to take it home, study it, and try to think of more topics.

(*e*) On the following day the children were assigned to groups of six. Each group then elected a leader and secretary and decided on a topic.

In two groups the individuals could not agree on a topic. These children re-arranged themselves and formed three groups of four individuals interested in a common topic.

(*f*) A visit was arranged to the A.B.C. studios, where the pupils saw a play being rehearsed and later heard it put over the air. They also visited a radio factory and saw all stages of radio production.

The liaison officer between the A.B.C. and the Education Department, and also the personnel officer from the radio factory, came out to the school and addressed the children on radio script writing, radio production, jobs in the radio industry and conditions of work.

(*g*) Excursions, talks by visitors, and class lessons were spaced at intervals to present satiation of interest and to stimulate motivation.

(*h*) A strong motivating factor was the provision of a wire recorder. On completion of the programme, a spokesman from each group gave an account of the group's activities and this was recorded. When a play, a programme, or an interview had been prepared, the whole group participated in the recording.

(*i*) Each group had a separate project. During group work the teacher spent some time with each group. His aim was to enter into the discussion or activity and to be accepted as a group member. He then made his contribution to the group goal, and his advice was accepted on its merits. In this way he was able to give guidance without the appearance of autocratic control.

At regular intervals the groups were brought together and progress reports were given by the group spokesmen.

Assessment of Results

The feeling of achievement and satisfaction—the writing of a script for a play, having it recorded, and hearing it played back; the look on the face of a child when he first heard sound coming from a crystal set of his own making was worth seeing.

Incidental learning. The group had an immediate goal in view, e.g. the preparation of a talk on sound waves to be given to class-mates or to be recorded. Knowledge was gained, not because it was a task imposed by the teacher, but because it was necessary for the attainment of the goal.

Social climate. At the end of the programme a second sociometric test was given. Markedly similar changes were noted in the three grades. There was a marked decrease in the number of rejections, and an increase in the number of acceptances. In grade V the first test revealed no cross-sex choices, and every child rejected at least one other child. In the second test a number of cross-sex choices appeared and twelve children rejected no one. In the sixth grade of girls the first test revealed two isolates. The second test showed that both of these girls received one acceptance each.

The permissive atmosphere resulted in very friendly relationships between teachers and children, and among the children themselves. A lessening of tension and aggression was shown by the decrease in the number of rejections.

Attitudes and Initiative

At first the children constantly sought direction. But gradually initiative increased. Instead of asking the teacher for information, a child would be observed searching through books, or studying a model to see how to proceed. Rowdy behaviour, such as calling across to other groups, was noticeable at first, but as the children became used to the conditions, they worked more quietly. Indeed, members of one group often asked another to be quiet, because, they said, 'we want to work'.

Group Work in Arithmetic

The doubt most often expressed by teachers concerns the practicability of using work-group methods in arithmetic. As a matter of fact, it is in this subject that the most striking academic results have been obtained.

The objections that are raised probably stem from a consideration of the convenience of the teacher. He fears that he may be involved in more preparation, more corrections, and more complicated supervision. He prefers the formal class lesson, followed by a series of similar daily exercises, and he often insists that all children do the same amount and the same kind of work each day. Soon the stage is reached when some of the pupils know the work thoroughly, while others have not yet grasped the principles involved. The class as a whole is not yet ready to go on to new work, so all are held back. This procedure is difficult to justify.

The teacher who decides to use work-group methods may follow one of two courses:

(*a*) He may have all groups doing the same type of work, in which case, provision must be made for the brighter children by having sufficient work of a challenging nature to keep them occupied. This may take the form of extra work on the blackboard, exercises from a text book, or practical assignments which stimulate interest.

(*b*) Groups may be allowed to proceed at their own pace and go on to new work when they have demonstrated, e.g. by passing a test, that they have a thorough grasp of the old work.

The most convenient size of groups for arithmetic appears to be four individuals. When assigning children to their groups, the teacher should consider the advisability of taking into account both sociometric choices and levels of ability. The children of a homogeneous group may be expected to keep pace with each other. This has a stimulating effect and overcomes the frustration and tension caused by the feeling of being left behind.

Each group may have a chart on which individuals record their daily output. This is a strong incentive, as the children soon become interested in improving their own output and that of the group.

Group Methods in English

Some aspects of English can best be treated with the class as a whole, for example, poetry; but others lend themselves ideally to group treatment.

In reading for content, each group can be assigned a portion of the material and set to prepare a summary. A spokesman from each group can then relate to the whole class the prepared statement. Debates between groups, short 'lectures' prepared by the group, and the writing of plays and stories are other activities suitable for group methods.

A. P. Ward and L. J. Murphy

The Establishment of a Democratic Atmosphere

Chapters 4 and 5 pointed out that the great value of fostering a democratic atmosphere in the classroom is that children receive early and realistic training in developing that understanding of the needs of others which leads to self-discipline, and which is essential for maintaining a democratic society.

A democratic atmosphere can be, and often is, established in a classroom without the use of group methods. Even with traditional class teaching methods the children may be allowed to take part in discussions for the purpose of planning their own activities, setting their own goals, and getting an overall picture of the purpose of their work; and the teacher may be a participating member rather than an authoritarian figure imposing assignments and sanctions on his subjects.

On the other hand, the mere introduction of group methods does not mean that a democratic atmosphere is automatically established. It is conceivable that a teacher might introduce group methods simply because he considered them to be the latest fashion, yet continue to use his authoritarian methods of control.

If a democratic atmosphere can be established in the traditional classroom set-up, why need the teacher bother with sociometric techniques and group methods? Some of the advantages of these methods are listed below:

When children work in smaller groups, the shy child will make contributions where he will be silent in the large group.

The isolate, or the rejected child, can be absorbed into a group of well-adjusted children who do not reject them.

These small, homogeneous groups form excellent nuclei for the introduction of activity programmes. (See Section 'Work Groups and Activity Programmes'.)

Group work enables children to co-operate *for the attainment of group goals.*

Greater opportunities are provided *for the attainment of individual goals,* and by contributing to group goals, children who set themselves high standards and have high skill or ability, or both, not only have the satisfaction of receiving recognition for their efforts, they are also encouraged to work to the fullest extent of their capacity.

The Development of Social Skills

Personality, built on the inherited bases of physique, temperament, and intellect, develops as a result of experience in social groups. It should, therefore, be an important function of the school to provide experiences which will contribute to the all-round development of the child.

An important class of experiences is working together to achieve a common goal. Individual interests become merged in the activities of the group, and the emphasis is shifted from individual competition to co-operation.

The pupils thus learn some important social skills, such as self-discipline, co-operation, unselfishness, and the ability to get on with others and to help others. The development of social skills is of great importance for personal adjustment.

The ability to communicate ideas and feelings freely is essential for mental health. One of the most significant trends in education to-day is the increasing importance which is being assigned to oral expression. It is heartening to see that time-tables allot more and more time to 'Morning Discussion', 'Oral Composition', 'Speech Training', and 'Dramatization'.

Group work gives more children a chance to speak, and the shy child is not as diffident as when he has to speak before a larger audience. The problem of a noisy room is one that may be solved by group decision. The matter is discussed with the class as a whole. Some understanding is reached as to what is a reasonable amount of noise and what should be done to correct people who are not co-operating. It has been found effective to allow any child in the room to go to the front, ring the bell and say to the class: 'We are too noisy, our group cannot work'.

Emotional Development

Various studies have shown that some of the most pressing worries and anxieties of primary school children arise in the school situation. For example, children in the sixth grade were found to suffer anxieties about health, bodily suffering or injury, school marks and promotion. By the time adolescence is reached, these anxieties remain, but the emphasis has shifted to fears centred on social situations—clothes, appearance, the impression made on others, and being accepted as members of a group.

During both stages the attitudes and values of the child's peers are more important to his development than are the attitudes and values of his teachers or parents. The quality of a child's emotional development at school, therefore, is determined by the quality of his social relations. The stable child is one who establishes stable relations with his own peer group. The timid child is one who is afraid to establish relations with his own peer group. The anti-social child is one whose attitudes and values diverge from those of his peer group.

The personality of the child is developed in the process of inter-action between the child and his group. The way the child sees him-self is a reflection of how he thinks his group sees him. Hence, as we are concerned with the mental health of individual children, we must consider each child's adjustment to his own group.

By using sociometric techniques to organize the class into work-groups, and by establishing a democratic atmosphere, the child's classroom environment can thus be controlled so that optimum conditions for his growth are provided. By allowing children to work in groups, the teacher brings into action powerful motivating forces, for in the group situation social needs can be satisfied—recognition, prestige, self-expression, security, and a feeling of be-longing—all may find fulfilment. In this atmosphere the child can develop his self-esteem, and grow to emotional and social maturity.

In the authoritarian atmosphere, in which the most commonly used form of motivation is competition, there results a struggle for status and leadership, which fosters self-centredness. When this atti-tude is widespread in the community, it results in tensions, frustra-tion, and aggression.

Academic Achievement

Though much has to be done before an exact answer to the ques-tion of the effect of group methods on academic achievement can be given it is possible to indicate what it is likely to be. The evidence suggests strongly that the results achieved by group work are at least equal to those secured by other methods; in fact in most cases they have been shown to be better. Here is one example of a study with typical results.

The investigation referred to in the section: 'How to form Groups —Use of Criteria': involved two fifth grades. One grade was taught arithmetic by the traditional classroom methods, while in the experimental grade the children were grouped as explained above. Before the experiment began, both grades were given the A.C.E.R. Otis Intermediate Intelligence Test and Form A of the A.C.E.R. Arithmetic Achievement Tests, Parts 1–6. No significant differences were found in the average scores of the two grades.

In the grade doing group work, the teacher put arithmetic exercises on the board each day for all children to attempt. At the beginning of the period, each group set itself a goal—the number of sums to be completed by the members of the group—but each child worked at his own pace, and there was no limit to the number of sums he might do. The teacher soon found that it was impossible to put enough work on the board to keep the brighter children fully employed, and to make sure that their work was properly corrected. These children after completing the blackboard exercises were allowed to work from arithmetic text books, and to correct their own work from answer books. The teacher was able to give a good deal of his time to the slower pupils, and children were at liberty to ask help of any other child, or to go out as a group to the blackboard for the purpose of solving a problem, either by themselves or with the help of the teacher.

At the end of four months, Form B of the A.C.E.R. Arithmetic Achievement Tests, Parts 1–6, was administered to both the grades. The grade doing group work had made *greater gains on all parts of the test to an extent that proved statistically significant.* In the experimental grade, three children had raised their arithmetical age by over twelve months, and five children had raised theirs by nine to eleven months.

Examinations. One interesting effect which has been observed several times is that under these conditions of classroom management the pupils will themselves ask to have examination papers set in order to assure themselves of their having made progress. If group

103

discussions produce this request by agreement, the best thing for the teacher to do is to set a paper and then leave the class to it. They will do their own marking and will discuss the results. Often they are too strict, and the teacher can use this to point out the general purposes of an examination and the criteria which are considered by examiners to be important or trivial, depending on the subject and the purpose of the particular examination. (See Chapter 9.)

A note to the Student. It is recommended that you now re-read Chapter 3 and follow up some of the more important references listed at its end.

VII

Psychological Tests and Testing

C. H. DOUBAY AND G. DOUGLAS

Synopsis

NUMEROUS tests are available to help teachers. They are, broadly, of three kinds: tests of cognitive ability or 'intelligence', achievement, and aptitude. Main attention in this chapter is given to the first two. It answers many questions about such tests and outlines what use can be made of test results for the more efficient organization of teaching and the benefit of individuals.

Why administer tests?

A teacher with an ordinary class of about forty pupils may have some sixteen 'average' pupils, six or seven in each of the 'slightly above' and 'slightly below' average groups, three or four 'dull' pupils, and five or six 'bright' pupils.

It is important that the teacher should know the category into which each of his pupils falls, so that he can ensure that they are not given tasks which are too far above or below their level of ability. Frustration usually results from both situations and this leads to aggressive behaviour, which is seen in its active form as impudence, quarrelling, destructiveness or other anti-social behaviour, and in it, passive form as boredom, which is so often mistaken for 'lazinesss' 'lack of concentration' and 'being easily distracted'.

C. H. Doubay and G. Douglas

A teacher also needs to know the levels of mental ability when some degree of homogeneity in a group is desired, as well as on those occasions when he may have to assess the work of his pupils in terms of 'capacity' or 'best effort'.

Knowledge of a child's mental ability level (in addition to other things) is needed in order to give educational and vocational guidance (see Chapter 10). It must be stressed that psychological testing should be carried out for the express purpose of assisting the child to adjust to the school situation and not for the purpose of obtaining discrete snippets of information about him.

Some teachers claim that they do not require the help of psychological tests to assess the mental level of their pupils. Whilst agreeing that some teachers are able to do this much better than others, experimenters have shown that, in general, teachers are not very successful at the task when dealing with normal children, and may be quite astray with children who are emotionally disturbed. Age is frequently overlooked and older and younger children are thought of as having equal levels of mental ability when they perform at equal educational levels in school; others tend to regard the child with ready speech, pleasing address, and other indicators of good social adjustment as necessarily possessing high mental ability.

It is not unusual in psychological clinics to find that problem children who have been dubbed as 'dull' by several teachers are really quite bright, while children who have been sent for examination on account of suspected 'dullness' are backward educationally solely owing to emotional maladjustment, not to lack of ability.

Despite the fact that most teachers will have obtained a certain amount of information about the child's mental ability from incidental observations, there is ample evidence to support the contention that tests should be used whenever possible to obtain unbiased, objective assessments of the child's *capacity* to learn, at the time of testing.

What kinds of tests are there?

There are tests of *cognitive ability, aptitude,* and *achievement.* Tests of cognitive ability, or 'intelligence tests', measure the child's general capacity to learn, his ability to profit from education. Aptitude tests measure capacity to learn in some limited fields of

Psychological Tests and Testing

education, e.g. music, art, languages, mechanical training. Achievement tests determine not capacity, but content. They may be in the form of 'Standardized Attainment Tests', which are designed to find out how much a person knows or what he can do, or in the form of 'Diagnostic Tests', which are designed to uncover differential weaknesses in attainments.

Any test which is given to one person at a time is called an 'individual test'; a test given to a number of persons simultaneously is called a 'group test'. If a test is to be done within certain time limits it is known as a 'speed test'; if time is unlimited it is known as a 'power test'. Some tests are in a verbal medium (Verbal Test), others have a pictorial content (Non-Verbal Test), whilst still others require the manipulation of objects (Performance Test). There are tests designed for very young children (Pre-School Tests), others for grown-ups (Adult Tests), and still others which extend over the whole range of human mental ability. It should be clear that any given test can be placed simultaneously in several categories based upon content, form, use, and range. To select the right sort of test for any given situation requires appropriate training in psychology and familiarity with the content of tests.

In schools, the group test is most frequently used since it saves time and expense. Usually several group tests will be given in a testing programme; in this case they are referred to as a 'battery' of tests. An individual test is used when the psychologist considers that a group test may not give a reliable indication of a pupil's ability.

How many tests are available?

There are more group tests of intelligence and attainment than individual tests. The results of aptitude tests should be accepted with more caution than those of other tests. Diagnostic tests are becoming increasingly important.

At present comparatively few good individual intelligence tests exist. The reason for this is not hard to find. To produce such a test requires considerable financial backing and the services of a team of trained psychologists and statisticians working for a long period. It required ten years to build what is probably the best known and most widely used individual test, the 'Revised Stanford Binet Scale'.

Even the construction of a group test requires considerable

107

financial backing and expert assistance at all stages of its construction. Furthermore, tests produced in one country cannot simply be taken over and used in another without a good deal of investigation to determine their suitability.

Test construction is thus a complex process, and this limits the number of tests available for any particular purpose. Each year, however, more tests become available and constant alteration and revision of existing tests is being carried out.

How is an intelligence test made?

This section is not meant to assist potential test constructors, but rather to give a brief outline of the process so that teachers will be in a better position to understand both the value and the limitations of tests.

Some general idea of what is involved may be gained from the procedure used in preparing a test of aptitude for learning Morse code. In the first instance a number of things that seemed to indicate aptitude were selected. They were combined into a test and tried out on trainees. Then by continual refinement, the test was left with only those items which were found to have been good predictors for those who succeeded in learning the code. It is in much the same manner that an intelligence test is evolved, but it must be borne in mind that the abilities which are tested by an Academic Aptitude Test are far more complex than those which go to make up a Code Operator Test. Consequently the construction of such a test is considerably more difficult.

Since it is not possible to test every aspect of a child's intelligent behaviour by a single test, certain tasks must be selected which will be a representative sample of such behaviour. From these, other aspects which were not sampled should then be capable of being predicted.

To ascertain which are the most suitable tasks is a long process. The first difficulty is to select *valid* items, i.e. those which retarded children or slow learners find more difficult to solve than do accelerated children or rapid learners, and which the average older child can solve more easily than the average younger child. It is also important that the degree of difficulty of the items should be considered—they should be neither too difficult nor too easy. Further, the constructor has to make sure that his test is *reliable*—that a child, on being retested shortly afterwards, will obtain the same result.

When, after repeated trial with different samples, the validity and the reliability of the test satisfy the constructor, there arises the problem of determining the average score of pupils at the various age levels. These scores are known as the 'test *norms*'. In order to obtain norms, the final form of the test has to be tried out on a large sample of children in the age ranges for which the test is to be used. By taking the various ages in turn and examining all the relevant scores it is possible to calculate the typical score for any given age. The norms are then used to evaluate the performance of any child who does the test. If he gets the typical score for his age (or one very close to it) he is considered to be of average intelligence. If he gets a score which is typical of some other age group (either older or younger than his own) he is considered to have the same mental ability as average members of that group. The child who gets the score appropriate to older children should be able to cope with the same school work as those older children; on the other hand, the child who gets a score appropriate to younger children will be able to work only as well as these younger children.

The score which the child obtains on the test (the *raw score*) does not mean very much, since it may be merely a number such as 21, 86, 52. The person who is using the test may not know whether, say, 52 represents a poor or a good performance, unless he has some standard against which to compare it. Since the test constructor has previously determined the scores which are typical for the various age groups, the tester can examine them to find out in which age group this score of 52 is to be found.

This leads to the concept of '*mental age*'—a term which signifies that the child who gets a score which is typical of some particular age group is regarded as having the same mental maturity (for this test) as members of that group. Thus a child of seven years who obtains a score which is typical of eight-year-old children is said to have a mental age of eight years. However, as the purpose of the test was to find out how well the child would perform at school, the term 'mental age' is merely another name for his score on the test. Nevertheless, this form of naming the score makes it more easily understood.

It is convenient to calculate the ratio of the score which the child

C. H. Doubay and G. Douglas

actually obtained to the score which he would have obtained had his performance been average. When converted into a percentage this ratio is known as the 'intelligence quotient'.

For instance, a child of twelve who performs at the average level for his age, will have a 'mental age' of twelve and a chronological age of twelve. His I.Q. is then:

$$\frac{\text{Mental Age}}{\text{Chronological Age}} \times 100 = 100$$

If he performs as well as a child aged nine, his I.Q. =

$$\frac{9}{12} \times 100 = 75.$$

The higher this quotient or percentage, the brighter the child and the more easily he should be able to deal with school work appropriate to his chronological age. Similarly the lower the percentage the duller the child and the more difficult it is for him to cope with school work. It must be stressed that 'intelligence quotient' (I.Q.) is merely a convenient ratio of test scores which gives some indication of the rate at which we may expect a child to learn at school. It refers to a performance on a particular test. It is likely, not only that the child's performance on another intelligence test would give a slightly different I.Q., but even that retesting with the original test may give a different result. (However, tests are constructed to give as much agreement as possible on retest as well as between different tests.)

How good are Intelligence Tests?

This is a question which is frequently asked—particularly by the teacher who has had access to test results and has found that several different I.Q.s are ascribed to the one child.

This question cannot be answered easily. The test user must be aware of several sources of error which can affect the accuracy of the test as a measuring instrument. In constructing and using a test it is assumed that the children are making their best possible efforts. This assumption may be false for any given individuals, for whom, therefore, the prediction will be less accurate.

110

Psychological Tests and Testing

The test items are limited to a comparatively small sample of the total number of intellectual tasks which the child can perform, and such limitation is also likely to introduce error because the child's abilities may have been affected by, for instance, special teaching. Similarly, limitation of the number of children upon whom the test was originally tried out to only a sample of the total child population may introduce another source of error if the sample selected was not truly representative of the population, or conversely, if the child tested came from some very out of the way group.

Test constructors are well aware of these possible sources of error and are able to give an indication of the amount of error to be expected in a score. Not all teachers, however, are aware of the 'probable error' of tests and many are inclined to think that if two tests give I.Q.s of 96 and 106 for the same pupil, the tests are quite unreliable or at least of very little value; whereas the discrepancy could be accounted for by the degree of inexactness, or 'tolerance', of the tests.

Every instrument has its own limits of error. If one repeatedly measures the length of a line with a ruler, no two measurements will be *exactly* the same. The physicist allows for this by taking the mean measurement and calculating the limits of error on either side. The same holds true in principle of a psychological test.

The important question is, 'Does the admission that there are errors in test scores destroy the value of the tests?'

When it is realized that I.Q.s are ratios obtained from inexact scores (the actual score and the expected score) and therefore must be inexact themselves, it will be realized that it is quite unrealistic to ask a pyschologist for the child's 'real' I.Q.

In practical educational guidance the school pyschologist would be unable to make different suggestions for the educational placement of two pupils whose I.Q. scores are 94 and 106 respectively, if he were working from test scores alone (which, of course, he should never do). Both pupils would be considered 'normal', i.e. likely to progress through school at the same rate, other things being equal. However, if examination of the school record of the two pupils suggested that there is a real difference between their learning rates, the psychologist would probably wish to find out whether the score of 94 represented the very best effort of one pupil or 106 the poorest score of the other.

C. H. Doubay and G. Douglas

In such a case he would probably administer another test (usually an individual test) in order to examine more closely the child's response pattern, and thus to arrive at a better assessment of the individual's potentialities.

Administering a Group Test

Organizations which construct psychological tests often make group tests available to teachers. If one aims to make the best use of the test the next important point to consider is: Who should administer the test?

The fact that some group tests are labelled 'self-administering' suggests that it is immaterial who administers them; in fact it appears that the individual could use the test on himself. The term 'self-administering' is used to distinguish it from individual tests, in which each item is read out or shown to the person being tested and the tester writes down the answers. In the group tests, the pupils write down the answers on the answer sheets.

The teacher should not be misled by such labels—the administration of a group test requires both skill and experience and should not be undertaken lightly by any person if he hopes to obtain valid results. Admittedly manuals which accompany group tests tell the tester what to say and when to say it, but more than mere repetition of the given formula is required.

The instructions are an essential part of the test. They must be given in the same manner as they were given by the test constructors when the norms of the test were being established. Synchronizing of 'timing' and 'instructing' requires complete familiarity with the test; thus the person to give the test should be completely familiar with the procedure of giving it—this familiarity is acquired by first practising and discarding the results.

Another part of the test situation which must be standardized is the social relationship between the tester and the tested. This relationship is called 'rapport'; it is an easy social situation in which the subject is motivated to do well but feels that the attitude of the examiner is one of impartiality.

The role of the tester is difficult for a teacher not only because the teacher may have fixed attitudes to the child to be tested but also because the role of 'subject' is made impossible for the child, since

112

he in turn will probably have fixed attitudes to the teacher. Close contact between teacher and pupil leads to the development of relationships which may be far from impartial. The presence of the class teacher in the group test situation may cause one child to exert himself to the limit of his ability; it may cause another child to give up even before the test has begun.

A further drawback to the teacher-tester role is the danger that the teacher may unconsciously assist the child. There is no suggestion here that the teacher may attempt deliberately to thwart the true purpose of the test; but it is true that help may be both given and received without either of the parties being aware that this is what has happened. The teacher who patrols the files of desks perhaps glancing over pupils' shoulders soon becomes aware of the quality of individual responses. Pupils who are accustomed to interpreting a teacher's demeanour as praise and blame can find cues as to how they are faring and whether their responses need checking.

There are also practical difficulties in the way of the teacher administering tests. If a testing programme is to be worth while, not a single test but a battery must be given—perhaps two general ability tests together with an attainment test in the basic subjects of reading and arithmetic. Such a battery is likely to take a full morning and to leave the teacher with a mass of correcting to do.

Co-operation of the school authorities must be obtained since some of the requirements of testing cannot be met in the ordinary classroom, e.g. the instruction that pupils must sit one to a seat. Testing times may disorganize recess periods and these may have to be arranged. Noisy classes which usually work close at hand may have to be cancelled for the occasion and the children sent to work with different teachers. Thus the teacher who wishes to test may have to arrange not only his own work but that of other teachers also.

All the reasons which are set out above suggest that it is the school counsellor, not the teacher, who should conduct group tests. It is well worth while for the interested teacher to make application to the authorities in his school system to have the testing of his class carried out by a psychologist who works in the schools. The teacher can then be confident that the results will be more reliable, and will give a better picture of the abilities and attainments of his pupils.

C. H. Doubay and G. Douglas

Miscellaneous Questions about Psychological Testing

We shall suspend the orderly development of the chapter here to deal with some of the peripheral questions that are often asked about testing.

Testing Very Young Children

The testing of very young children except in unusual circumstances is not desirable. Research evidence indicates that the relationship between results secured before children reach six years of age and those found later is not very high. In many cases they can be very misleading.

Sometimes this is due, no doubt, to the difficulties of testing very young children. Written verbal tests cannot be used, rapport is often hard to establish, motivation may be poor even with the few tests that are used, and situations sometimes arise which baffle even the most skilled psychologist.

Testing Children with Sensory Defects, e.g. Deaf Children

There are tests for use with children who have sensory defects. Most of them are performance tests which do not depend upon verbal skill to the same extent as the usual tests of intelligence. The testing of atypical children is a task for trained psychologists and the average results are usually below those for normal children.

The Effect of Illness on Test Results

Minor dispositions appear to have little influence on test results. A child's intelligence test results are remarkably constant even though some of them may have been achieved under comparatively adverse physical conditions.

The Effect of Schooling on Test Results

Examination of the items of tests which are in common use will reveal that the test constructor has made the assumption that the child is receiving the normal education of his place and time. Practically all items involving facility in dealing with words and figures are affected by schooling, but this is no drawback to the value of the tests since the assumption is quite correct in practically all places where the tests are likely to be in regular use.

114

Psychological Tests and Testing

However, there are cases in which, for some reason or other, a child has not received normal schooling. The teacher should make a careful note of the child's educational deficiencies and of the circumstances that surround them. The psychologist will then be in a position to estimate whether the usual intelligence tests do give a true measure of the child's ability. If he decides that they do not, he will probably give the child individual non-verbal tests in which school achievement plays a less significant part. Pictorial and performance tests to which reference was made earlier might well be employed. In passing, it is worth noting that these non-verbal tests, the instructions for which are communicated in pantomime to the child, may be used with children who speak no English.

The Effect of Coaching on Test Results

The practice of coaching children to answer intelligence tests is very widespread in countries where the results are used for selecting students for different types of education. The practice is, to say the least, unprofessional. It arises out of the misuse of the tests for examinations and in selection, whereas their real purpose is for individual counselling.

That performance can be improved has been demonstrated many times, but the results secured are invalid and useless.

Achievement Tests

Many of the ideas used in the construction of achievement tests are derived from those originally employed in the development of intelligence tests.

Achievement tests measure how much has been learned, not, as do intelligence tests, what is the capacity for learning. A test which sets out to find out how much a person knows, or what he can do, is usually called a 'standard attainment test'; a test which is designed to uncover weaknesses in attainments is known as a 'diagnostic test'. This nomenclature is not standardized and it sometimes is necessary to inspect an 'achievement test' to see into which category it falls.

Teachers set examinations to assess attainments in various subjects. The difficulties, drawbacks, and misinterpretations involved

C. H. Doubay and G. Douglas

are discussed at length in Chapter 9. However, it is likely that the discussion of the reliability, validity and error-terms of intelligence tests will have caused the thoughtful teacher to wonder whether these factors also need to be considered in classroom examinations.

The aim of standardized attainment tests is to remove some of the weaknesses of the school examination. However, these objective measures do not differ materially from those used by the teacher except that they have been carefully constructed and scientifically standardized upon representative samples of pupils. A further advantage of these tests is that they are methods of measurement which are widely applicable and which provide valid comparisons from child to child and school to school. They reduce the subjective element in tests—instructions for giving them, marking them and assessing their results have been standardized, in consequence their reliability and comparative values are relatively high.

What Ideas Lie Behind the Achievement (Attainment) Test?

Theoretically, the best way of determining what a child knows about some subject, say arithmetic, would be to examine every piece of work he had done in this subject in his time at school. Since this is manifestly impossible, certain items are examined which are considered representative of the components of the course which the child has done.

Having this sample of the items in the school curriculum in a given subject, the teacher prepares an examination for all the children in the school system; those who are able to get many of the items correct know a good deal about the subject, those who get few items correct know comparatively little.

As in the case of the intelligence test it would be possible to develop age norms—the average number of correct responses to be expected at a given age, or grade norms—the average number of correct responses for the average child of a given grade. Further it would be possible to derive an 'educational quotient' in that subject similar to the intelligence quotient by converting to a percentage the ratio of a child's actual score to the expected score for one of his age. By means of this concept of 'educational age' or quotient it would be possible to compare a child, not only with the other members of

116

Psychological Tests and Testing

his class at school, but with children in other schools; there would also be comparisons of grades and schools.

However, no achievement test can live up to the ideal that has been laid down—chiefly because the construction of the test involves the accumulation of errors, similar to those occurring in the construction of an intelligence test, but usually much larger. Unless this 'error' is kept in mind the various norms which are supplied with the test are likely to be spurious and to suggest that the discriminative powers of the test are much finer than they are.

Further Difficulties in Expression of Achievement

To be of use, norms must be presented in a manner that is meaningful to teachers. Some of the terms used, e.g. 'average nine-year-old' or 'average grade VI child', are not as simple as they appear at first sight. Unless a teacher has had long experience in teaching a certain grade, he has probably little conception how 'the average grade III child' performs, since there are wide variations in performance between children, between schools, and even between geographical areas. The same is true for the expression 'average nine year-old'. Statistical abstractions are mistaken for children and teachers are deceived into believing that they know what the score means.

Again, there is confusion when norms using the word 'average' are applied to completed skills and to uncompleted skills. Reading could be termed a completed skill—once a child has grasped the mechanics of reading he can go on and on, provided suitable reading material is at hand; thus some children in grade IV can handle reading material of grade VI. Arithmetic, on the other hand, is an uncompleted skill—in most schools the child can proceed only after the teacher has shown him how to make the next move. Thus a child may be able to multiply by decimals but be completely unable to divide by them; and it is unusual for a child to be able to attempt any of the arithmetic of a higher grade. Now the teacher sees 'the average grade VI reader' as a child who is able to perform up to average class level, but what can 'the average grade VI child' do at arithmetic? He does not know everything the teacher has tried to teach him, nor does the 'very good child', since a mark of 10 out of 10 is rare in examinations. The reader may care to work out what his impression would be of a child who was tested at mid-year and stated to be of 'average grade VI standard'.

These points have been made not to decry the value of standardized attainment tests but to draw the attention of teachers to some of the difficulties in their use and to help them realize that such tests are not infallible and inexorable assessors. In conclusion, one more cautionary note—if a school curriculum changes and items of the curriculum are allotted to other grades the grade norms of the test will obviously be less valid than previously.

Diagnostic Achievement Tests

An excellent description of the diagnostic test is given in F. J. Schonell, *Individual Difficulties in Arithmetic:* 'A diagnostic test in any school subject is constructed for the specific purpose of analyzing the exact nature of the progress made by pupils in each important aspect of the subject. The test takes into consideration all the vital skills involved in each important aspect and these are tested by a series of carefully graded examples which cover all important steps in the acquirement of the skill. Thus a diagnostic test differs from an ordinary classroom test and from a standardized scholastic test in so far as its main object is to analyze, not to assess.'

The standardized attainment test result is expressed in terms of 'norms', from which one can tell whether the child is 'poor', 'very good', etc., in that subject. The teacher might be well aware of those pupils who are 'poor at the subject' but the result of the standardized test does not show the reason, though the marker who marked the child's paper would be able to gain some ideas (e.g. from a very untidy set of answers).

The diagnostic test concentrates upon this aspect of the subject— thus a diagnostic test of reading disability would have sections dealing with accuracy of word recognition, nature of the pupil's attack on words, type of visual errors made, use of context for word recognition, and ability to discriminate words. A diagnostic test in subtraction would begin with a simple subtraction, one digit from another, and end with a four figure subtraction involving the ability to borrow and to cope with zero in either the top or the bottom line. Once the teacher has located the child's stumbling block he can proceed to remove it.

118

Psychological Tests and Testing

Not only does the diagnostic test assist the teacher to find the difficulties of the individual child, but it helps the teacher to make periods devoted to revision more useful. Some children are kept revising work in which they are already quite competent, whilst others who have difficulties are being kept at the wrong type of work. The diagnostic test shows for each child what wants revising.

Thus the diagnostic test is a tool for the teacher. Unlike the standardized test it can be applied quite informally, nor need all the class be tested at the one time. If just one child is failing consistently in a certain branch of a subject the teacher can get the child to do the test at some appropriate time. The teacher who can locate and remove a child's difficulty is likely to be repaid by an improved attitude of the child to the whole classroom situation.

What use can be made of the Test Results?

This is the crucial question for the practising teacher. Unless he can be supplied with a satisfactory answer it is not likely that he will be enthusiastic about having testing carried out in his class or be co-operative whilst it is being done. The discussion of achievement tests was undertaken before attempting to answer this question in order to provide enough evidence first.

In every grade there are children whose progress cannot be considered satisfactory. What additional information can psychological tests give?

(a) *The child of 'very poor ability'*. This child may already be one year retarded through having repeated a grade lower down in the school. His school career has been a long series of failures which may have engendered hostile attitudes in teachers and towards teachers. Testing, particularly when several tests have been used over a period of time, may indicate that the cause of the child's difficulties is his lack of ability for the routine school work, and that even with the best endeavours of the child and the teacher he is not likely to go very far. Some education authorities make special provision for such children and provide them with a modified curriculum so that their educational development is not carried on in an aura of failure. Even when such a child remains in the ordinary class, the teacher can at least rest assured that the child's shortcomings are not due to deficiencies which can be overcome by 'better concentration', 'greater

119

application', or 'developing a better attitude'. In such a case a modified class curriculum may not only be an advantage for the child but a fuller understanding of the child's difficulties may also lead to an improved attitude towards him on the part of the teacher.

(b) *The child who is unduly accelerated.* Although the school curriculum is presumably designed for children of a given age it often happens that a child begins school a year or more before the statutory age. Where social adjustment is good, the home background co-operative, and older brothers and sisters ready to give assistance, such children often make a very good start at school. However, it often happens that after three or four years such children are in the doldrums. The child who was once dubbed 'a bright little thing' now appears dull. Testing will often indicate that such a child has average ability but is attempting to cope with school work suited to children a year older. Examination of achievement test results often indicates all-round weaknesses in the basic subjects of reading and arithmetic.

The teacher is then in a position to recommend the repetition of a grade to return the child to its correct mental age group. He is also in a position to explain to the parents and to the child why this recommendation is being made: that the repetition is an important stage in the education of the child and not a punishment for badly done work. Further, the teacher is in a better position to influence parents who are over-eager to start their children at school.

(c) *The child who 'achieves significantly below his ability'.* Here it is necessary to begin with a warning. It is easy to think that if a child has 'average' ability his performance in his school subjects should be 'average' too. However, the ability to succeed in the basic subjects of the curriculum and intelligence test ratings are not as closely related as people often think they are. Opportunity (home influence, teaching) and emotional influences (attitude to school, stability, social participation) are even more important.

Where, on teacher's examinations and on standardized tests, the attainments of a child of at least average ability are shown to be well below those of his class, the teacher may use diagnostic tests in order to determine whether difficulties are located in the *material* of the curriculum. If they are not, it will pay the teacher to look to the other influences which affect school progess. How does the child fit into the child-groups which form the class? Are the teaching methods autocratic or democratic? What is the home background of the child? The teacher may have to get to know the parents.

It will be seen that psychological testing can take the teacher behind the stereotypes of 'laziness' or poor concentration and set him on the track of the real causes. If the teacher is unable to locate the cause he should make sure that he records his investigations and impressions. The child who is unable to make the grade at school is a problem child, one who is in need of assistance.

(d) *The child whose ability is 'well above average'.* In every grade there are children who have sufficient mental ability to cope with the work of a higher grade. It often happens that the achievements of these children are quite mediocre. At school their abilities have never been challenged by their tasks; their teachers do not always think of them as being particularly bright even though they seem to be able to pass examinations without much effort.

It is not always desirable that these children should be in the grade to which their mental ability entitles them. Mental ability is only one of the factors involved in grade placement. But since these children are likely to do well not only at secondary education, but at tertiary, too, it is essential that the school should use and develop their latent energy.

Conclusion

The findings of social psychology indicate that the classroom group should be broken up in order to free the children to develop social skills as a basis for learning. The findings of psychological testing re-echo the warning that to treat a class of school children as an undifferentiated mass is unrealistic. There are wide differences in ability and in achievements in the basic subjects of the curriculum; hence the arranging of a syllabus into class-lesson units on the assumption that the material can be delivered to children in 'lesson-loads' is in conflict with the facts of the situation.

Comparison of the current reading material of a class with that in a standardized reading test will show that some of the children are wasting their time on reading matter that is actually years below their powers of comprehension; maybe they are 'watching the place' whilst some child of poor ability and poorer reading skill 'barks at print', swift silent readers with wide vocabulary but poor emotional adjustments are tensely awaiting the misery of having to read aloud; children with specific reading disabilities—undiagnosed and un-remedied—have 'lost the place' and so lose their turn to read. It is clear that the process is largely a meaningless time-wasting ritual—and it should be kept in mind that the 'meaninglessness of reading, is one of the causes of poor ability in reading.

Standardized reading tests results will suggest to teachers which children are eligible for membership of groups that are doing assign-ments or carrying out projects which involve reading from texts in the school or class library; the tests will also indicate those children whose reading achievement requires closer investigation. This in-vestigation will be made easier by the fact that the teacher has no longer to waste his time over children for whom the reading lesson was too easy and that he will be in a position to know to which chil-dren he can give responsibilities for assisting the weaker readers. Further examination of intelligence test results in conjunction with reading test results will indicate which children are likely to experi-ence difficulty with the normal reading matter of the class on account of low general ability. These children can be grouped and provided with reading material more suited to their ability.

A procedure which makes reading more meaningful by allowing the child to achieve social satisfactions through purposeful group membership, by using success rather than failure as the incentive, by seeking out and removing the causes of failure, is an excellent method of securing an all-round improvement in the reading ability of all members of the class.

Summing up

The aim of this chapter has been to show how psychological testing can help to supply the teacher with the information he needs if the child is to undergo the maximum of worth-while personality development during his school days and if the teacher is to enjoy the satisfaction that comes from doing a job that needs doing. It has attempted to show the strengths of tests so that teachers will respect them, and also their weaknesses so that teachers will not be misled by them. Above all it has attempted to show that tests can be powerful tools for helping the teacher to do more efficiently what he is doing already, and more effectively as regards the long-term aims of education.

SELECTED REFERENCES FOR FURTHER READING

Some of the basic ideas in intelligence testing are discussed in the preliminary sections of the two following books:

1. TERMAN, L. M., and MERRILL, M. A., *Measuring Intelligence* (London Harrap, Army Edition).
2. WECHSLER, DAVID, *The Measurement of Adult Intelligence* (New York, Williams & Wilkins, 3rd edn., 1944).
3. CARMICHAEL, L., (ed.), *Manual of Child Psychology* (New York, Wiley, 1946).
   The following chapters are especially relevant:
   Goodenough, Florence, 'The Measurement of Mental Growth in Childhood'.
   Miles, C. C., 'Gifted Children'.
   Jones, Harold E., 'Environmental Influences on Mental Development'.
4. SCHONELL, FRED J., *Diagnosis of Individual Difficulties in Arithmetic* (London, Oliver & Boyd, 1937, 2nd edn., 1942).
The following deals with reading, spelling and composition:
5. SCHONELL, FRED J., *Backwardness in the Basic Subjects* (London, Oliver & Boyd, 4th edn., 1949).
6. CATELL, R. B., *A Guide to Mental Testing* (London, University of London Press, 1936), 2nd edn. 1948.
7. *Studies in Reading*, Vol. 2 (Scottish Council for Research in Education, London University Press, 1950). This contains a valuable three-page summary of the main reading deficiencies, their diagnosis, and remedial suggestions.
8. An excellent survey, with a thoughtful and provocative introduction to the problem of selection for higher schools, is Stephenson, William, *Testing Schoolchildren* (London, Longmans Green, 1949).
9. VERNON, PHILIP E., *The Measurement of Abilities* (London, University of London Press, 1940). This is a fairly advanced text for those who wish to go more thoroughly into the method of test construction. It also contains excellent chapters on how to test and on examinations.

VIII

The Problem Child

F. L. ROUCH

Synopsis

PREVIOUS chapters have considered the need for classroom procedures which will enable the teacher to create and maintain a healthier spirit of peer group relations. The traditional teacher-centred and subject-centred methods tend to make the child feel that learning at school is a coercive process, and quite different from learning outside school. With group methods, the pupil's feeling of being coerced is replaced by one of co-operativeness through collaboration with his equals; and the teacher, having been seen as a disciplinarian, is now seen as a friendly helper who wants the same things as the groups. Consequently, the timid, isolated child finds it easier to learn and to enjoy social interaction, and the 'problem child', having nothing to rebel against in the school, learns to work out his problems by achieving greater stability in one of the most important regions of his day-to-day life.

Nevertheless, problems remain, partly because of physical or home conditions outside the teacher's control, partly because deviant behaviour has become so strong a habit that some special steps need to be taken to correct and restrain it. The following chapter is designed to give the teacher some aids for detecting cases in which individual rather than group treatment becomes necessary.

The Problem Child

An important aim of this book is to emphasize that a school class is made up of a number of individual children, each one being different from the others in general mental ability, in home background, in attitudes and interests, in emotional reaction, and in a host of other ways. Some implications of these individual differences have been discussed, as have certain organizational and teaching methods which might facilitate the development of each unique personality to the fullest possible extent. This chapter is intended to help the teacher with some of the problems associated with the 'problem child'.

The term 'problem child' does not cover a discrete classification into which children can be neatly assigned. It entails the notion of degree, rather than kind, and is used to describe a child who is assessed as having deviated noticeably from a standard of behaviour which is accepted as being 'normal' or 'desirable' by a particular individual, or group of individuals.

Many children who require a detailed psychological examination are readily observed by the teacher; in some cases the deviant behaviour is ever-present, ever-disturbing. However, it is also important that a problem child who might normally remain undetected should be discovered and treated—for example, the isolate who remains unnoticed because she is popular with teacher and works well in class; the child who successfully covers up a gnawing emotional conflict under a cheery external façade; or the bright lad whose light is hidden under a bushel of poor academic attainment. These problems can usually be discovered only by using suitable techniques for assessing personality.

A problem case should be approached objectively, and any urge to make moral valuations should be repressed. A problem child is not wicked or innately bad. He is a child who is adjusting to a set of forces in a particular manner.

Those who deal with problem children should treat, not the symptoms, but the underlying cause of the symptoms. If the cause remains, the eradication of one kind of undesirable reactions will almost inevitably be followed by another kind, the consequences of which may be even more undesirable. One should not ask, 'How can Mary be stopped from stealing?' but 'What is causing Mary to steal?'

F. L. Rouch

Many children can be helped with their problems if they can discuss them with their teachers. In simple cases, a direct approach to the child is usually successful. When the child might not be prepared to give information fully, he could be approached—at least for a start —indirectly. Thus if the undesirable adjustment appears to be due to faulty school relations, a Moreno test might be given to the class; or the class might be asked to write, on an unsigned sheet of paper, the main 'grouches' they hold against the teacher, school, or other schoolchildren. With encouragement, they will respond to these techniques.

Types of Problems and Suggested Treatment

Problems will be classified under four main headings:

(a) Problems related to intellectual and academic development.

(b) Problems related to personality or behaviour disorders.

(c) Problems related to physical factors.

(d) Emotional problems, psychoneuroses, and psychoses (that is gross personality disturbances).

The usefulness of this classification is limited, because in many cases there is much overlap between categories. An instance is the case of a lad who is backward in his school work. Largely for this reason, he dislikes school, is inattentive in class, and plays truant whenever possible so that he can attend to more interesting pursuits. To cover up his actions, he finds it necessary to lie.

Thus, because of the inter-relation between various aspects (each of which in itself could be regarded as problem behaviour), one would require a picture of the sum total of forces acting on the child before any of the facets could be satisfactorily remedied.

(a) *Problems Related to Mental and Academic Development*

Few teachers are fully aware of the ranges of age and ability amongst the children of their grade, and the implications of these ranges. The following figures drawn from a sixth grade of sixty-seven children are by no means atypical of sixth grades.

In May (the month of calculation) the chronological age range was from 10 years 1 month to 13 years 5 months—an age range of 3 years 4 months. The range of assessed mental age was even greater, being more than six years. The mental age of the brightest child was calculated at 15 years 6 months.

It is true that amongst children in the lower grades there would generally be greater homogeneity of chronological and mental ages. It is true also that in the above grade, a few dull children and one very bright child are largely responsible for the greater part of the disparity—the majority of the grade would fall within a much narrower range of age and ability. Nevertheless the fact remains that every child in a grade has to be taught.

Many behaviour problems in the classroom are directly related to the failure of the teacher to take into account adequately the individual differences in age and ability. A child cannot be expected to remain interested and to attend closely to what is being taught, if under the conditions obtaining at a given time it is not possible for him to cope with the work of the grade. On the other hand, the bright child who finds the grade rate of progress too slow, often worries the teacher by inattention or distracting behaviour.

By using the group method of teaching (as discussed in Chapters 4 to 6), many of these difficulties can be solved. But some special problems warrant further comment:

(i) *Mental backwardness.* Extreme cases of mental backwardness are generally associated with some bodily disorder. These include glandular disorders, infections of the nervous system, or conditions like mongolism, and others. As a rule, such children are confined to an institution or kept at home.

The Education Departments provide special education for two groups of mentally backward children. Both types of schooling strongly emphasize the practical and social (as distinct from the academic) aspects of education. Selection of pupils is dependent largely upon an assessment of intelligence; but secondary factors, such as social and personality requirements, are also considered. Those children in Victoria whose assessed I.Q. falls within the 50–70 range may be admitted to a 'Special School'; those within the 70–85 I.Q. range are eligible for entry into an 'Opportunity Grade' within an ordinary school.

In addition to these children, there are usually a number of slow-learners—the plodders, the ones who require a great deal of explanation and practice. In large classes, especially, these children present

F. L. Rouch

the teacher with a difficult problem. There is little point in forcing them along at the pace set by the average child of the grade; yet the teacher should lead them at a sufficiently stimulating rate.

In dealing with this problem, it is important for teachers to avoid the tendency to regard mental backwardness as something innate, unchangeable, final. Except in those cases in which mental backwardness is attributed to gross bodily disorders, it can be safely assumed that the level of a child's mental development is largely dependent upon the external conditions which operate on him throughout his life. If these conditions (e.g. socio-economic background, family pressures, level of motivation) remain comparatively constant over a period of time, it is likely that the child's level of mental development and his assessed I.Q. will likewise remain relatively constant. Research has shown, however, that a radical change in external conditions can lead to considerable changes in mental ability and in I.Q. assessments.

Just as the roots of a child's anti-social behaviour should be sought in his environment, so the roots of mental backwardness should be sought in environment. For instance, parents differ enormously in the amount of pressure they exert on the child in the matter of his academic achievement, and in the help and guidance they give to him in his studies. In many cases, the forces operating on the child might be beyond the teacher's manipulation. His efforts might fail, for example, to lift the child above the depressing effects of a poor home background. Nevertheless, he should endeavour to remain constantly optimistic that he may effect important changes in some of his less mentally bright children.

The promotion of slow learners needs to be in the form of a compromise between the standard of academic achievement reached, and a consideration of emotional and social factors—it being generally desirable to grade children approximately according to chronological age. Because of the importance of these factors, the Psychology Branch of the Victorian Education Department advises that retardation should not exceed eighteen months, except in special circumstances. In these cases adjustment could be helped by providing social contact with children of their own age during such periods as sport, art, or handwork.

(ii) *Very bright children.* The very quick learner also presents a

128

problem. In principle, the solution to this problem is similar to that of teaching any child. It lies in stimulating interest, and in restricting progress as little as possible. This entails providing, and allowing him to provide, sufficient work to keep him interested and occupied; encouraging him to expand beyond the limits of his routine grade work, with individual or group tasks; guiding his activities along educationally or socially useful channels suited to his ability; or in general, assisting him to use and to develop fully his above-average capabilities and potentialities.

Provision of these opportunities for the bright child is likely to maintain his interest in school work, and to reduce the likelihood of his becoming a nuisance as a result of having too little to do to keep him happily busy. It is likely, too, to give him little chance of adopting the idea that he does not need to try very hard, that everything is easy.

To grade a bright child more in keeping with his ability level, it is sometimes desirable to allow him a certain amount of accelerated promotion—acceleration should, however, be recommended only after due consideration of the child's level of achievement, his physical size, the level of his emotional and social development, and other factors which might be relevant. The Psychology Branch of the Victorian Education Department advises only in exceptional circumstances that acceleration should be allowed to exceed eighteen months.

(iii) *Educational backwardness.* If a child is backward in all or some school subjects, it is important to determine the factors which are probably responsible for his backwardness, so that the most suitable way of helping him can be discovered.

Too often educational backwardness is explained in terms of the child having inherited a smaller capacity to learn, with the subsequent implication that little, if anything, can be done to increase his rate of learning. However, if mental backwardness is, as we have seen, so largely due to environmental influences, how much more is this the case with specific educational backwardness?

There are many factors which could cause a child to achieve a standard lower than the expected average. Perhaps the most important are those associated with socio-economic background, and home pressures arising from this background. On the whole, working class parents tend to place much less stress on the importance of academic achievement than do middle class parents. This is not surprising, because academic qualifications are much less important for gaining entry to working class occupations. These parental influences may be exerted quite unconsciously in the form of modes of speech, reading habits, leisure-time activities, and so on.

Other factors associated with educational backwardness are a late start at school, irregular school attendance, physical or sensory handicaps, emotional disturbances, lack of interest in particular subjects and many others.

Once the teacher is satisfied that there is a straightforward explanation—such as an educational history involving frequent changes of school, without any further complications—remedial treatment can commence. However, if the cause is more subtle, it will usually be necessary to treat the cause and the effect simultaneously. The opinion of a psychologist should be sought in the more serious cases.

Even in the absence of complications, it is most necessary for the child to regain interest in the work, and confidence in his ability to attack the subject successfully, before the backwardness can be successfully tackled. It is thus essential for him to begin the remedial work at or about his present level of achievement, and to progress at a pace suited to him. Suitably graded supplementary books in reading, arithmetic, and other school work are invaluable for creating interest and confidence; and these can be selected, to a certain extent, to make use of the child's hobbies or interests, so that motivation reaches a high level.

The problem of giving one child, or a few children, individual attention when a whole grade has to be taught, can be simplified if activity work is introduced (e.g. 'Read and Make', 'Find the Answer'); or if the children could be assisted in their work by a classmate who is advanced in the particular subject, and is socially accepted by them. To ensure acceptance, it would be preferable for them to choose their own helper. Here again the importance of sociometric grouping in the classroom is apparent.

(b) *Problems Related to Personality or Behaviour Disorders*

Under this classification may be listed a group of problems related more to psychological than to physical factors, and which are probably more in accord with the popular conception of the term 'problem child'. Included in this group are problems associated with abnormal emotional reactions. Although there are wide variations in what could be regarded as normal emotional behaviour in a given situation, there are two groups of reaction which indicate underlying psychological factors that need investigation. Firstly, there are those responses which are highly emotional and out of all proportion to what might normally be expected in the circumstances—such as the child who stamps her foot, throws away her bat, and argues volubly when fairly caught out during a game. Secondly, there are those in which little or no emotional reaction is shown, under conditions in which emotional responses could normally be expected—for instance, the child who shows no reaction whatsoever when his particular group is excited about winning a competition.

Again it is necessary to bear in mind that to consider isolated problems and their origins is to some extent artificial, yet it must be done for expediency. Not only do all problems merge into each other, but it is common to find children whose symptoms fall within several of the categories to be described below. The importance of accumulating a detailed picture of the child's background cannot be overemphasized.

The following are some of the problems which are likely to be encountered in the school.

(i) *The inattentive and 'lazy' child.* The general problem of motivation has been discussed in Chapter 3, and references have been made to the inattentive and 'lazy' child in sections of the present chapter. Nevertheless referrals are so often marked 'lazy', 'unable to concentrate', 'will not apply himself to school work', that it may be helpful to discuss separately some aspects of this problem.

Inability to cope with the standard of work set is easily the most common factor in cases of inattention. The physical state of a child at the time is also important. If a child is suffering from physical ill-health, inadequate rest and sleep, or from under-nourishment, his span of concentration is likely to be affected. Over-active children, too, tend to be distractible and to flit from task to task.

Next, there are factors which are more psychological: The child who is preoccupied with disturbances at home; the child who escapes from the difficult and unpleasant situation at school by planning leisure-time activities; the day-dreamer who compensates for feelings of inadequacy or frustration through fantasies of success. It is not uncommon to find that the inattention of an over-indulged child results from the discrepancy between the amount of freedom enjoyed at home and that allowed at school.

The inattentive older child who is bored with school life generally, and who has his mind set upon leaving school and earning a living as soon as possible, poses a different problem. Here the solution would appear to depend largely upon the teacher's skill in changing the child's attitude, in arousing his interest by providing him with immediate goals towards which to strive, by relating school work to everyday needs and activities. The problem is closely connected with curriculum reform. For instance, a lad who is about to leave school to become a grocer's assistant sees little reason why he should listen attentively to lessons on algebraic equations.

This example raises an important point, full discussion of which would require too much space. This is, the relation of the behaviour patterns in the child's own socio-economic class to the behaviour patterns required of him at school. The question is referred to in Chapter 1. Briefly, the child at school is expected by the teacher to conform to middle class patterns and values. These include punctuality, neatness, orderliness, and submissiveness to authority. But some children may not be accustomed to any of these at home and on the streets. Another pattern concerns cleanliness, and the higher value placed on 'white collar' work than on manual work by the middle class, and, of course, by the teacher, who is himself a clerk (in the old sense of the word). Unless the teacher is aware of these differences in social behaviours, he will be the cause of much misunderstanding and conflict in the child.

(ii) *Stealing.* The term stealing is usually so strongly associated with the notion of conscious wrong-doing, that it might be well to point out that stealing has little or no moral meaning to young children. Even though some parents might attempt to train their children in the general code of honesty, it is not until a child has reached a certain stage of mental and social development that he is able to differentiate between his property rights and those of others, or to understand why he cannot take a thing which he would like to have. Amongst older children stealing can be an unconscious act, a manifestation of some serious disturbance in emotional stability.

As in other types of problem behaviour, the underlying causes must be discovered before the symptoms can be treated.

Some cases of stealing can be directly traced to a lack of example and training in the home. A few parents, of course, set a standard of dishonesty which their children simply imitate. But well-meaning parents can also unwittingly encourage their children to have little regard for other people's property rights. If, for instance, they are free and easy about the family's possessions, their child cannot be expected to worry whether a desired article belongs to him or not; or if his possessions are used or given away regardless of his desires or permission, he is likely to believe that he is entitled to do likewise with the property of others. The Chicago studies have shown that this is the case among the very poor in the slums.

A different type of stealing is closely related to the child's emotional life. A sense of insecurity, arising from discord in the home, sibling jealousy, or lack of parental affection, might lead a child to steal as a symbolic attempt to build up his security. In these cases hoarding of articles is not uncommon. Sometimes an isolate will steal in order to buy sweets with which he hopes to gain the favour of other children. Sometimes stealing is a way of 'getting even' with those who have been teasing, criticizing, or in other ways upsetting his adjustment. Hence, to deal with the problem, it is important to examine a whole range of forces—both conscious and unconscious—which might be acting on the child.

Apart from obviating the more general emotional thorns, specific steps should be taken to change the child's attitude. For instance, he might be assured of receiving regular pocket money each week; or he might be shown how he can use his spare time in interesting, constructive pursuits. Above all, he must be given a sense of being trusted; and efforts must be made to build up his self-respect, to eliminate his resentment towards his fellows, and to have him accepted by a group.

(iii) *Telling lies.* Lying is another problem behaviour about which moral judgments are especially frequent. Psychologically, a child who lies is regarded either as going through a normal phase of

133

F. L. Rouch

development, or as one who is not adjusting satisfactorily to his environment.

In young children the demarcation between the world of reality and the world of fantasy is not sharp. Their uncertain memory, inaccurate notion of time, concepts of events and things vastly different from those of an adult, and vivid imagination, make it understandable that misinterpretations of fact are common at this age. They might well believe that 'Teddy wet the floor' or that they saw 'Fairies at the bottom of the garden'. This phase, up to the age of five to seven years, should be regarded as normal, and it is important that the young child should not be made self-conscious about telling that kind of untruth. Little, if any, advantage would be gained; and besides disturbing the child's perception of his world, one runs the risk that he might be given the first suggestion that he is able to use words to deceive.

Conscious lies are symptoms of maladjustment, and are therefore more serious.

Perhaps the most common cause of conscious lying is fear of consequences, as in the case of the child telling a lie in an attempt to escape from punishment, either moral or physical. If the fear is removed, this type of lying is likely to cease.

Lying also provides a means of compensating for feelings of inadequacy or rejection. The backward child might build up stories about his skill at catching rabbits. The child who lacks attention at home might gain consolation from making other children believe tales about the wondrous kindness showered upon him by his parents. Or perhaps he will seek attention by the more direct method of deliberately lying in order to get a hiding for it—any attention being better than none.

The child can adopt the habit of lying from simple imitation of adults, many of whom use without compunction false statements, to guide, threaten, coerce, and compel the child.

This enumeration of a few of the more common causes of lying serves to illustrate that the problem is complex. If one understands the reasons why lies are told one is in a more favourable position to remedy the causes and remove the necessity for lying. Punishment and badgering are to be avoided. Of course, it is necessary to point out to the child (if he is old enough) the desirability of telling the truth and to reward him for doing so rather than punish him for

134

lying; but unless the causes are removed, 'lectures' will have little effect. In the home it might be that the child needs greater affection from the parents, or a less rigid discipline. If the cause is in the school environment, the child needs to be helped to overcome his school difficulties and to develop a different attitude towards them. For example, if fear is the major factor, the teacher might adopt a more approachable manner with the children, or if lying is an attempt to overcome feelings of isolation, the child could be drawn more closely into group activity.

When the lying habit has become well-established it might take a long time to effect improvement. In other cases new attitudes develop rapidly.

(iv) *Truancy*. Sometimes, absence from school without legal excuse is beyond the child's control. He might be kept home to mind younger children, to run messages, or to help with the family chores. In rarer cases, his absence might be due to the inability of his parents to provide him with the necessary clothing or footwear. When such factors can be excluded, the reasons for the child's general dislike of school, or for his dissatisfaction with certain aspects of school life, need to be investigated.

Inability to cope with school work is a common cause of truancy, especially when such inability has led to unsatisfactory teacher-child relationships. The disparity between the freedom enjoyed at home and that allowed at school, a disinclination to accept the dull character of certain classroom lessons, resentment at being, in his opinion, punished unfairly, and an urge to leave school in order to earn adult status and a living, are factors which might affect a child's general dislike of school and so lead to truancy. With others, truancy is more an escape from particular aspects of school life. For example, a child who likes school work might stay away from school to avoid unpleasant situations caused through poor peer-group relations, or to avoid taking part in organized sport.

Treatment should endeavour to eliminate the factors causing truancy. The appropriate action, of course, would depend on the individual case. It might necessitate action to impress upon the parents the need to allow the child to attend school regularly. The child might require remedial tuition in backward subjects, or placement in a grade for mentally retarded children. Adjustments in school, peer-group, or home relations might be needed. Fortunately, over recent years, the trend in dealing with cases of truancy has been towards acquiring an understanding of the psychological factors involved. Punishment and parental fines appear to be losing their popularity as 'remedies'.

(v) *Speech disorders.* Only a few of the more common types of speech disorders to be found amongst school children can be dealt with here.

In the vast majority of cases, children can talk intelligently long before they begin school. If a child cannot speak normally by the time he commences school, his case should be investigated. Two common causes of tardy speech development are mental retardation, and deafness. Also, if there is a family history or late speech development, a child of average intelligence might not speak normally until he is six or seven years of age.

Dyslalia is the speech disorder which is also known as 'baby-talk'. The child can understand what is said to him, and can express himself, but his speech is unintelligible. Although dyslalia can result from several factors, emotional factors usually predominate. The disorder is often present in children who have a sense of insecurity because there are jealousy, fear, and disharmony in the home. It is also found in children who are 'babied' by over-protective mothers; or it might be the result of lack of parental interest in talking to the child and helping him to develop normal speech.

Stammering also results from several causes, both physical and psychological. Treatment, as in other cases of speech defect, needs to be carried out by a specialist; but the following points might be a useful guide to the teacher.

A very young child might stammer and be unaware of it. The words 'stutter' and 'stammer' should not be mentioned to the child. He should never be asked to stop and start again, or to speak slowly, or to take a deep breath, or be subjected to the dozens of other aggravations which people mete out. Once a child is made aware that his stammer is socially unpleasant, further trouble is likely to occur. It might be as well to explain to the other children that he must not be taunted because of it. It is unwise to make one who stammers badly read aloud by himself in front of the class, although reading in unison should do him no harm. Finally, it is well to remember that an example of quiet, smooth, calm, easy speech set by teachers and parents can do much to overcome a tendency to stammer in the young child.

When stammering is a symptom of repressed, unconscious aggression, it is best dealt with in a psychological clinic.

The treatment of speech disorders needs to be carried out by specialists, with, of course, the co-operation of the parents and school usually in a Speech Therapy Clinic. Before children are recommended for speech therapy they are given a medical examination to determine the extent to which physical factors are responsible. In most cases they are referred also for a psychological examination.

(vi) *The attention seekers.* Every teacher has come across the problem of the 'attention seeker'.

In milder forms, the symptoms might be offers to do helpful tasks, such as cleaning the blackboard, dusting the desks, or some other way of trying to gain the teacher's approval. (A certain amount of this type of behaviour could be expected from any child. Whether it constitutes abnormal behaviour would depend upon the frequency and insistence of offering help.) But in more serious cases, the child is apt to become a constant source of distraction both to the teacher and to the class. He might consistently arrive late, persistently ask irrelevant questions, talk and clown during lessons, fidget—in fact do anything in order to have the limelight thrown upon him, even if the limelight takes the form of reprimand or punishment.

This type of behaviour is usually, a façade to conceal deeper feelings of insecurity. Although a child might appear to be popular with his peer-group, investigation might disclose that he feels insecure in his relations with them. He might lack sufficient love and attention in the home, or the showing-off may be an attempt to prove to himself that he does not mind not being able to achieve as well as the other children.

The attention seekers are a nuisance, but rejection only makes their problem worse. The teacher must attempt to understand the child's social background, at home and at school, before he begins the weaning process.

(vii) *Enuresis and masturbation.* Lack of bladder control and excessive manipulation of the genital regions are both not uncommon in younger school children. Both are symptoms of rather deep seated emotional disturbances (though enuresis may also have physical causes). In both cases it is vitally important not to punish the child or in other ways call attention to his behaviour, but to have the child psychologically and, if necessary, medically examined.

(c) *Problems Related to Physical Factors*

It is not intended to discuss the problems relating to physical factors as fully as those involving the more purely psychological factors. Cases of physical disorders should be referred to an appropriate medical centre.

However, the teacher might find helpful a discussion of some of the consequences of having physical problems.

(i) *Physical defects and deformities.* School children are notorious for the lack of mercy they show to the child who is handicapped by unusual physical features. They are only too ready to apply nicknames, to mimic defective speech or gait, and at times to extend their persecution even to the point of physical cruelty.

The seriously handicapped child is usually faced with sufficient cause for psychological disturbances, without being disturbed further by the ridicule—or even comment—of others. Any form of persecution, therefore, should be actively discouraged at school. A discussion with the other children often proves effective. It is important to help the child not to overestimate his handicap, and to prevent him from trading on the sympathy of others. These could probably be best achieved by treating him, as far as possible, as a normal child— handling him firmly but with understanding, whilst making due allowance for his reduced skills.

Although totally deaf or blind children are unlikely to be encountered in normal schools, many cases of milder sensory defects are met but are frequently not recognized as such. Any case in which partial deafness or visual handicap is suspected should be referred at once for special examination.

The microphone of the hearing-aid is usually worn under the child's outer clothing in a position near the chest. For full efficiency the apparatus needs to receive sound waves as directly as possible. Thus if the desk in which the child is sitting is too high in relation to the sitting height of his body, or if many children are seated in front of him, the sound waves are blocked, and the effectiveness of the aid is diminished. For this reason, it is preferable for the child to sit at, or near, the front of the class. At times it is necessary to adjust the volume of the hearing aid, and allowance should be made for any 'fiddling' associated with this adjusting.

Children with weak eyesight would also benefit from being seated close to the blackboard, so that eye-strain is reduced to a minimum. Adequate lighting, and blackboards that are not shiny, are, of course, necessary for all children.

(ii) *Left-handedness.* The problem of whether a left-handed child should be converted to right-handedness often confronts teachers and parents. No rigid rules can be laid down as to the advisability of changing handedness. Each case needs to be considered on its own merits.

During recent years the wisdom of changing the handedness of a child has been questioned. Some investigators hold that changing over can cause speech defects and emotional disturbances; others say that the method of inducing the change, rather than the change itself, is responsible for any undesirable effects. However, all agree that a child should never be teased or forced into using his right hand.

One may ask whether change is necessary. It is true that the majority of people are right-handed, and that much equipment is designed for the right-handed person. But in sport, industry, and commerce very few examples can be given to substantiate the belief that left-handedness is a serious disadvantage. In everyday life the extent to which we use our unfavoured hand is seldom realized. Nevertheless, change is probably advantageous if it can be made with ease and without unfavourable consequences.

In young children, in whom hand dominance is not firmly established, change can usually be effected without complications. However, before commencing the training, the teacher should seek the approval and co-operation of the parents to ensure that efforts are co-ordinated at home and at school.

In some cases it would probably be unwise to attempt change. Children (especially older ones) who strongly favour their left hand should generally be allowed to continue left-handed; whilst it would also be unwise to attempt to alter the handedness of backward or emotionally unstable children, who are in sufficient difficulty without being further burdened.

F. L. Rouch

In the classroom it is preferable for the left-handed child to sit so that the light comes over his right shoulder. If dual desks are in use, friction can be reduced to a minimum by allowing him to sit on the left-hand side of his neighbour.

Training in penmanship is often facilitated in the early stages by tracing or copying letters. The easiest and most natural slant should be encouraged, even though this might mean the adoption of back-hand. When pens are used they should be held well back from the nib and the hand kept below the base-line to avoid smudging.

(d) *Psychoneurosis and Psychosis*

The psychoneuroses are a group of psychological disorders, not as severe as insanity, which usually have outward and visible signs of serious mental and social conflict. Their discussion is beyond the scope of this book.

THE FUNCTION OF THE PSYCHOLOGIST

(a) *When Should a Case be Referred to a Specialist?*

The question might be asked, 'Which problem cases should a teacher attempt to handle?' and 'When should a case be handed on to a specialist?'

The answer to both questions will depend on several factors: the experience and skill of a teacher in detecting and handling such cases; the assessed severity of the case; the amount of time a teacher can afford to give to the child; the psychological or medical facilities available to the district.

In general, however, the following types of problem cases should be referred to a specialist for investigation and recommendation:

(i) Cases in which physical factors are suspected.

(ii) Educationally backward or mentally retarded children for whom special education is considered desirable.

(iii) Cases in which the personality or behaviour disorder appears to be due to deeply-rooted emotional disturbances.

The above categories should not restrict the range of problems about which expert advice is sought. Teachers would be wise to adopt as a maxim, 'When in doubt, refer'.

The Problem Child

Summary

The term 'problem child' has a wide range of meaning and emotional connotation to different people. Whether a child is regarded as a problem depends entirely upon the particular frame of reference within which the child's behaviour is judged, and upon the context in which the behaviour is observed.

Although some types of problem behaviour can be observed only too readily, other children who could benefit from psychological or psychiatric referral would most likely remain undetected unless they are discovered by the use of special techniques, some of which can be used by the teacher.

An objective approach to the problem is essential. Evaluating the child morally, and labelling him with 'problem tags', are to be avoided.

Problem behaviour is a symptom of disturbances in the child's life. The task, in all cases, should be to determine the causes of the behaviour, and to remove these causes. It is useless to treat the symptoms only, for even if one group of symptoms has been eradicated, another group of symptoms will almost inevitably follow while the underlying causes remain.

The teacher can do much to prevent some types of problems from arising, and can help to reduce the severity of problems which do arise. However, relations between the teacher and his class need to be friendly and 'democratic' before children will freely discuss their problems.

Cases which appear to involve physical factors, children for whom special education is thought desirable, and those in whom deeply-rooted emotional disturbances appear to be present, should be referred to a specialist for examination. The handling of other types of problem cases should be at the teacher's discretion, so long as he bears in mind the maxim, 'When in doubt, refer'.

SELECTED REFERENCES FOR FURTHER READING

1. BARTON HALL, M., *Psychiatric Examination of the School Child* (London, Edward Arnold, 1947). This book is probably rather advanced for teachers. It is more a guide to a psychologist or psychiatrist.

141

F. L. Rouch

2. BENJAMIN, Z., *The Emotional Problems of Childhood* (University of London Press, 1948). A useful book especially written for parents and, teachers.

3. BOWLEY, A. H., *Everyday Problems of the School Child* (London E. & S. Livingstone, 1948). An instructive book dealing with the everyday problems of a wide age-range of school children—from those attending the day nursery to those attending the secondary school.

4. BOWLEY, A. H., *Guiding the Normal Child* (New York, Philosophical Library, 1943). Of particular relevance to the present chapter are Chapters III, V and VI, which deal with difficulties related to the preschool period, to the middle years of childhood, and to the adolescent period respectively.

5. BÜHLER, CHARLOTTE; SMITTER, FAITH; RICHARDSON, SYBIL; BRADSHAW, FRANKLYN, *Childhood Problems and the Teacher* (London, Routledge & Kegan Paul, 1953). The analysis of behaviour problems shows the basic causes of individual disturbances and is extremely useful to teachers. Teachers will also derive help from the analysis of children's free creative activity. This is one of the few books that adequately define the role of the teacher with respect to the problems of children.

6. BUXBAUM, EDITH. Foreword by Anna Freud, *Your Child Makes Sense* (New York, International Universities Press, 1949). Although specifically written for parents, this book contains much material of value to the teacher. The last section deals exclusively with the child's need for group identification, both at home and at school. The author explains how delinquent behaviour in most cases reflects poor group adjustment.

7. CLEUGH, M. F. *Psychology in the Service of the School* (London Methuen, 1951). Written primarily for the use of parents and teachers this book contains a minimum of technical language and a large number of illustrative examples.

8. HYMES, J. L., *Teachers Listen, The Children Speak* (New York Committee on Mental Hygiene of the State Charities Aid Association, 105 East 22nd Street, New York 10.). A very good pamphlet on some of the problems a teacher meets and methods of approaching them.

9. JENKINS, GLADYS GARDNER; SHACTER, HELEN; BAUER, WILLIAM W, *These are Your Children* (New York, Scott, Foresman and Company N.D.). Written in simple language, it gives the basic stages in development of school-age children. Each age has its special problems and the authors have indicated how the teacher can best cope with the needs of the normal and the atypical child.

10. RIDENOUR, N., and JOHNSON, I., (1947):
    i. *When a Child Hurts Other Children.*
    ii. *When a Child is Destructive.*
    iii. *When a Child Uses Bad Language.*

The Problem Child

iv. *When a Child Won't Share.*

v. *When a Child Still Sucks his Thumb.*

vi. *When a Child Still Wets.*

vii. *When a Child Masturbates.*

viii. *When a Child Has Fears.*

(New York City Committee on Mental Hygiene, 105 East 22nd Street, New York 10, N.Y.)

This is a series of pamphlets on special problems of children aged two to five years. Although they deal with young children, the pamphlets are valuable for all teachers and parents.

11. Teagarden, F. M., *Child Psychology for Professional Workers* (New York, Prentice-Hall, 1940). Much of the discussion in this book is of a technical nature and beyond the requirements of the teacher. However, Chapter XIII (The Child and his School) and Chapter XIV (Behaviour Difficulties) are of relevance to everyday teaching, as also are sections of other chapters.

12. Left-Handedness. *The Education Gazette* (*N.S.W.*) 44, **7**, 226-7. An excellent article for teachers.

13. *Advances in the Understanding of the Child* (London, The Home and School Council of Great Britain, 1935). A book comprising a series of articles and Study Group Outlines which were originally compiled as a basis for a year's study for parents, teachers, nurses, and others interested in bringing up children. A noteworthy feature of the book is its sound practical approach to the subjects discussed.

14. *The Education of Exceptional Children.* Forty-ninth Yearbook of the National Society for the Study of Education. Part II. (University of Chicago Press, 1950.)

IX

The Purpose and Conduct of
Examinations

P. LAFITTE and N. F. HOLT

Synopsis

EVALUATION is an important part of education. It is imperative
that examinations be integrated with the process of teaching and
learning, relevant to the content of teaching, and reliable. In the
light of present knowledge it is possible to offer advice to teachers on
each of these points.

Evaluation, however, goes far beyond examinations and takes into
account many other factors. To keep track of these, cumulative record cards are indispensable.

Introduction

In most education systems the traditional examination plays an
important role. To a certain extent, which varies from school to
school, and from one class to another, it is the chief criterion on
which a child is judged as having 'passed' or 'failed' in his year's
work, and on which a decision is reached whether he is to be promoted or not.

A continual assessment of the degree of success for each child is
an essential part of the educational process. Anything which can
be considered to be such an assessment is, strictly speaking. an

The Purpose and Conduct of Examinations

examination. Throughout this volume, methods of assessing various aspects of a child's school behaviour are discussed. In this chapter, the emphasis is more on the formal examination of acquired knowledge.

Tests serve various purposes. It is necessary to know where a child ranks on any subject in his own class group, or in the school population generally. It is also necessary to know the standard of a class group in relation to other classes and other schools. Also there is the 'diagnostic' use of examinations: their use in order to discover a pupil's strengths and weaknesses in knowledge and his interests and attitudes related to each school subject.

This chapter will be concerned with some of the weaknesses of the traditional examination and its usual applications.

It is essential to think clearly about the possible effects of examinations on the adjustment of the individual child and the purposes of education in general. The educational system often demands that the teacher should judge the work of his pupils by traditional examinations. The teacher, therefore, should be aware of the limitations of such examinations, their reliability, and the extent to which they measure the things that are important in the child's education.

In many secondary schools, especially the larger ones staffed with instructors who are experts in different subjects, the success of the work of the school is considered mainly in terms of the number of certificates and scholarships gained. In such schools much of the teaching is directed to training the pupils to answer the sort of questions expected in examination papers. In a highly competitive society this may be necessary. But, within the school, examinations must have a wider function. In general, they will be properly used if they are integrated with the flow of teaching and learning, relevant to the content of teaching, and reliable.

Integration

It is, unfortunately, easy for examinations to get out of line with the general aims of education.

(a) Some examinations are set by persons whose chief concern is to test the preparedness of entrants to an advanced course, for example a University course. These examinations may tend to break up the even flow of teaching by setting too much work, at too high a level.

(b) A similar difficulty is found where the work is limited to that

145

prescribed by the examinations. The annual examination generally has a powerful effect on the work of the secondary school. The rigid syllabus and the external examination (in its present form) and sometimes even the internal test, make it difficult for the teacher to exercise initiative and imagination in his work. Often he is forced to confine his teaching to instructing the class in the techniques needed to pass the examination.

These difficulties are even more marked where there are two or three annual public examinations which must be passed in turn. It is not enough that a few of the more able pupils go on to the higher levels, unless the others also gain.

The teacher can, of course, do little about these weaknesses of the public examination except to be aware that they are weaknesses and not to accept them as inevitable. Brereton (2) suggests that some of them might be overcome if teachers took a more direct part in setting public examinations. However, the difficulties mentioned illustrate something more general than this matter of procedure. Education, as Brereton argues, serves too many vaguely defined and probably conflicting purposes, so that there are bound to be clashes of interest not merely between the teacher and the examiner but also among the different ways in which the teacher might approach his task. Teachers look for many different things in examinations.

How often does the class teacher ask himself the meaning of a score of three out of ten for 'poetry' or 'art', or for that matter, almost any subject? All too often a score of ten for 'art' indicates an extremely neat drawing-book, filled with flower pots, vases, and an occasional piece of fruit, the dimensions of which are precisely the same as those in other children's books, due to the careful directions given by the teacher at the blackboard. Additional requirements for a high mark in these circumstances are that there are no dirty fingermarks and that all lines are drawn lightly.

What is true of art is true to a certain degree of all subjects. The usual type of written examination tests only certain aspects of education, and too often the unimportant ones. It tests mainly the efficiency of learning facts: about the grammar of a classical language, or about world history, or skill in spelling or in carrying out routine calculations in mathematics.

The worst effect of examination pressure on the pupil is that his education consists, to a serious extent, of cramming for examinations. To the extent to which this occurs, the average child has little chance of developing an interest in a subject for its own sake. When a subject has no intrinsic appeal to the child, and does not add something of value to the growing personality, it has little educative value even if he does pass an examination in it.

The implications of these ideas are described by Kandel (3), p. 159: 'The crucial problem of the day centres, therefore, not so much on the question of improving the machinery of examinations. As far as the individual pupil is concerned, he will be no better off educationally no matter how reliable may be the techniques by which he just manages to pass or fail. The ultimate question is the validity of the type of education from which he is capable of profiting.'

The problems of the integration of the public examination into education as a whole belong to the future. There is a miniature reflection of these problems that is of immediate practical importance for classroom examinations.

(c) The fairly common practice of setting frequent tests (up to weekly, or even twice a week) in the classroom serves only to disrupt education. It may be that this practice is an expression of anxiety on the part of the teacher; but it is true that a nervous child is worried by it. Behind this practice is the idea that children will not work unless they are pushed, driven, or lured on. This idea is in any case a confession of failure, for no child will be educated in desirable ways who does not accept the purpose of education. Besides this, the idea does not even work on its own level.

The syllabus is broken up into rigidly separated and poorly connected particles, which the pupil learns as for a radio quiz. The pupil can hardly help learning that knowledge is acquired for the sake of passing the weekly quiz and also (especially where the class is re-ordered after the weekly test) that passing examinations is one of the greatest goods in life. Such outcomes are incompatible with any serious educational purpose.

The internal test is within the control at least of the school and mostly of the class teacher, and the rule to be adopted is simple. The absolute minimum of class work in which progress must be separately tested for any practical purpose is defined by reference to the purposes of examinations: to test suitability for promotion, to test individual progress for diagnostic purposes, and perhaps to test the standing of the class at critical points during the year. Class tests are then restricted to this minimum and never taken beyond it.

Relevance

Relating the questions set in the examination to what has been taught is obviously important; moreover, it is not difficult. Two points about internal and class examinations may require attention.

(*a*) The questions should bear some relation to the time spent on teaching the various topics. This cannot be a rigid rule. Clearly a part of the syllabus which links two main topics and which amounts by itself to a twentieth of the year's work does not necessarily rate a twentieth of the examination. Other inequalities due to the relative difficulty of topics should also be accepted. However, it does happen that a teacher allows his enthusiasm for a particular part of the syllabus to outrun his discretion and therefore sets, say, two-thirds of the questions on one-third of the work. This practice is to be avoided. Apart from reducing the value of the examination as a test of progress, it may have unexpected repercussions, for children quickly learn to adapt their work to what the school's folklore reports of the teacher's habits.

(*b*) Questions should always be worded clearly and simply. The function of the question is to define for the pupil what parts of his knowledge he is to write down. Setting questions with a 'twist' in them requires the pupil to apply something he has learnt to something substantially different: that is, to produce a sudden flash of generalization or extension in the examination. If he has been taught to generalize or extend some particular point, formula, or process it is quite reasonable to examine him in order to see if he has learnt to do so. But to test whether he can do so in the examination with no previous teaching is irrelevant: it is not normally the purpose of examinations to test ingenuity or intelligence. The same goes for questions with 'trick' wording, where the pupil has to interpret what was in the teacher's mind and has a fair chance of answering the wrong question. The examination is not a test of ingenuity in mind-reading. The more often the pupil finds it being used for this purpose, the more likely he is to believe that developing this low grade social skill is an important aim of education.

148

The Purpose and Conduct of Examinations

Reliability

It is well known that examinations are unreliable because examiners mark inconsistently from time to time and from one to another. It has been claimed, indeed, that a mark in the usual kind of written examination reflects little more than the particular examiner's standard at the moment of marking. Examples of inconsistencies found in various investigations (such as **3, 4, 5, 6** and many others) are too numerous and too impressive to be disregarded. It is likely, however, that general conclusions about the intrinsic unreliability of examinations have been too hastily drawn. Many of the investigations were made under artificial experimental conditions that were quite unlike those of a school examination. Some investigations show that unreliability is not so general as may be supposed. The pioneer English investigation (**4**) in this field illustrates these points.

Experiments on the marking of School Certificate papers in several subjects all showed that the examiners taking part in the experiment disagreed in their placing of candidates and disagreed considerably in their standards. In the School Certificate English experiment, for example, the range of awards among seven experienced examiners marking forty-eight papers was from no failures to nineteen failures: and so for other awards. Similar results were found for other subjects. But disagreement in placing the candidates was less marked. In the Chemistry experiment, the data showed that the rank orders of the different examiners were in close agreement: it was only the final classing that was unreliable.

It is notable that this experiment was the nearest to being like a real examination: of the suggested conditions of reliability that are set out below, it met three, (*a*), (*c*), and (*d*). The Latin experiment, which met only conditions (*c*) and (*d*) as it was confined to papers that were all reputed to be worth a 'middling mark', showed more disagreement in the ranking of candidates than did the Chemistry experiment. The History experiment, which did not even meet conditions (*c*) and (*d*), showed even more disagreement.

This simple analysis of one set of experiments is, of course, far from sufficient to reverse the general finding that examinations are unreliable, but it does suggest a modification: that reliability depends on orderly conditions. Unfortunately, the investigations in this field have been little concerned with the analysis of different conditions: and this in itself is sufficient reason for treating the general finding with considerable reserve.

Until more detailed comparative analyses have been made, one can do no more than suggest six main conditions for reliable examining. These are inferred both from investigations and from experience of examining, and all are of importance to the practising teacher.

Six Main Conditions for Reliable Examining

(*a*) The papers to be marked by any examiner should have a full range of quality. This condition is important whenever more than one class does the same examination paper, as happens in the larger primary schools and with internal examinations in the secondary schools. In such cases it is important that the examiner should mark each question in turn right through the papers of all the classes concerned.

(*b*) The corollary condition is that every set of papers should be marked by two or more examiners, each taking a different part.

(*c*) The papers set must cover the syllabus adequately, as noted in the discussion of relevance, but must have no alternative or optional questions. Marking the same content for all papers is necessary for sound comparisons to be made. Papers allowing a wide choice, such as six of twenty questions, can easily produce as many different sets of answers as there are candidates; and then there is no basis for comparison.

(*d*) Marking criteria and systems should be discussed by all the examiners concerned. Whether or not this should go as far as constructing model answers and allocating part marks depends on the examination. At all events, there should be clear agreement on what is to be done before it is done.

(*e*) The marking system should give the greatest possible discrimination throughout its range: that is, it should be a flat ranking system. For example, with a test which is scored from one to ten and with two classes each of fifty pupils, it should be decided beforehand that, in each class, the best five pupils would score ten marks, the next best five would score nine marks, and so on down to the worst five, who would score one mark. With a simple ranking method such as this it is assumed that the different classes are of the same average standard. If this assumption cannot be made, some adjustments need to be carried out. It is not proposed to outline the various techniques in this chapter, as they are available in educational literature (e.g. **7**, **5**, pp. 48–50).

Besides giving better discrimination than the usual system which is heavily bunched round the middle marks, this system avoids the fallacies of both absolute and class marking. It is easy to decide that two answers differ in quality, but as Brereton (**2**) observes, it is not really possible to say that one is 60 per cent. of a perfect answer and the other only 50 per cent. Nor does it mean much to say that the poorer just passes and the better is well in: this judgment belongs to a later stage of marking.

(*f*) Papers are assessed as a whole by simply adding the ranks for questions. Classing the papers is a separate operation. As it is critically important, and is apparently the least reliable process in the examination, it is important that it should be done by all the examiners together, with full discussion of the criteria. The ranking system gets rid of the conventional 50 per cent pass mark and leaves the way open for inspection of the results. These will be well spread out, with little bunching in the middle, so that it will seldom be necessary to draw an arbitrary line between pass and failure, separating closely adjacent total marks. It should be clearly realized that the closer the critical marks are, the more arbitrary the line is. The teacher who, for instance, feels certain that a score of 48 per cent or even 45 per cent indicates failure (on the conventional criterion of 50 per cent to pass) is pressing hard a rather fine distinction even if the examination is known to be reliable.

The effect of ranking may be demonstrated by an actual case. A class of forty-five sat a second year university examination in which there were twelve parts. The parts were each marked on a flat ranking scale from 0 to 10 and were given equal weight, so that the total possible marks ranged from 0 to 120. The ranks were then converted mathematically into marks on a scale with the same range (so that the total possible marks still ranged from 0 to 120) but with the usual bunch in the middle. The table on p. 152 shows the distribution of the class (*a*) when ranks are summed (*b*) when bunched or modal marks are summed.

151

Total Marks	Distribution	
	(a)	(b)
115–124	1	
105–114	2	1
95–104	0	2
85–94	1	2
75–84	5	5
65–74	8	11
55–64	7	9
45–54	5	8
35–44	6	5
25–34	5	2
15–24	5	

The actual range of total marks from the summed ranks is 102 and from the bunched marks is 77. The superiority of the ranking method is especially useful at the bottom of the class. Of the forty-five candidates, nine failed; and in order to decide the pass/fail line it was necessary to consider the bottom fourteen candidates. For the summed ranks, these fourteen were spread over a range of twenty-six (from 15 to 40 total marks) and it was possible to draw the line in a gap, as total marks 31, 32 and 33 were not awarded to anyone. For the scale of conventional type, the bottom fourteen candidates would have been spread over a range of nineteen (from 30 to 48 total marks) and failing the bottom nine would have meant drawing the line between 45 and 46 total marks.

Classing the candidates

There are two general ways of fixing the line (or lines). With a large class, for which it can reasonably be assumed that quality does not vary from year to year, a fixed proportion may be passed. Brereton (2) in fact argues that as external or absolute standards are impossible this frankly arbitrary procedure should be generally adopted. On the other hand, it is often possible (and with small and variable classes is necessary) to make a judgment in terms of how much the candidate should know in order to go on to the next year's work. In this case the examiners work down to the last candidate they are prepared to let through, then up to the last they are not prepared to let through, and then close the gap, if there is one.

The Purpose and Conduct of Examinations

The discussion so far has been concerned only with ways of making the conventional essay-type examination more reliable. An important last point is that a discreet use of objective tests will increase reliability.

'Objective' tests

The basic notion underlying the so-called 'objective' test is that of formulating questions which can be scored absolutely reliably, that is to say, the same examiner on two different occasions or two different examiners must score each question in the same way.

One type is the 'True-False' question, in which a statement is answered with 'true' or 'false' or a question with 'Yes' or 'No'. For instance: 'A horse is a quadruped': True-False; 'The factors of $a^2 + b^2$ are $(a + b)(a-b)$': Yes-No. An extension of this type of question is the multiple-choice question in which several alternative answers are given. An answer is given by indicating one of the alternatives to be the correct answer. For instance:

A *Radian* is a

- (*a*) point on a circle
- (*b*) radius of a sphere
- (*c*) unit of angular measure
- (*d*) atomic particle
- (*e*) reflected light ray.

For subjects such as History, Social Studies, and English Literature in which the examining of facts is generally confused with the examining of appreciation and understanding, 'objective' tests can be used to test memory of facts learned and certain logical and discriminatory powers. For instance:

He guided the ship of State through stormy waters to

- (*a*) the summit of success
- (*b*) a successful conclusion
- (*c*) the end of the trail
- (*d*) a peaceful harbour
- (*e*) the fruits of victory.

Every teacher who is free to set his own tests should acquaint himself with the various forms of 'objective' tests, and the techniques of constructing and using them. Then he can proceed to use them to test aspects of his subjects which are not tested adequately by the essay-type question. Suitable texts on this topic are listed in the bibliography.

In subjects like History, English, and Social Studies, one exceedingly important advantage is that a pupil can be tested objectively for his knowledge of spelling, punctuation, and facts. His essay can then be separately assessed for qualities like style, continuity, and originality, which can be discussed with him. Marks assigned by teachers to an essay are mostly in fact compounded of marks for neatness and all the other aspects just mentioned, combined subjectively in varying proportions for different pupils.

Mention is made in Chapter 7, on psychological testing, of the 'standardized' attainment tests available from test publishing services. These tests can be of great value to the teacher who is interested in reliable assessment of the attainment of his pupils in their school courses.

It must be realized, of course, that while objective tests are a valuable means of simplifying and clarifying the examination procedure, they are by no means a complete substitute for the essay-type examination. They are useless by themselves in any subject that requires the argument of a case, or consecutive exposition, and with such subjects may even be misleading. The pupil presumably cannot expound the facts if he does not know them, where he can quite well know them without being able to expound them. A sole emphasis on the examination of isolated facts would lead again to the radio quiz type of education, which is reason enough for using objective tests with discretion.

The Cumulative Record

However much care is taken to integrate examinations with the general flow of education and to make them relevant and reliable, they give only a part of the information which is needed, and which can be gathered, for every pupil. If the educational process is to be evaluated at all fully, it is necessary to assess other things besides the learning of facts. Adequate assessment would answer among other things the following questions:

The Purpose and Conduct of Examinations

Has school life given the pupil an interest in acquiring knowledge for its own sake?

Does the social environment of the schoolroom promote the growth of a healthy personality in the child?

What have been the trends of development of personality, abilities, and interests in the child?

What do we know of the child's personal and social characteristics, his social and economic background?

Throughout this manual these matters have been discussed. They are all relevant to this chapter because examinations, in their broader sense, must test the extent to which these various aspects of the child's personality are developing soundly.

The Cumulative Record Card is a device used in many schools by means of which all the available information about each child is recorded during each year of his school life. On the record card are recorded all examination results, intelligence and other test results, health records, unusual accomplishments, mental, emotional, and physical experiences, extra-curricular experiences, athletic, social, and intellectual, vocational interests and plans, social adjustments, personality ratings.

The value of such information carefully, fully, and continuously recorded over a period of years lies in the use to which it can be put for educational and, later, vocational guidance. It is clearly superior for assessing a child, since all available information is used, rather than the results of one examination.

While an efficient system of records of this sort can best be used when the procedure is uniform throughout a school, the teacher can achieve much, even if he has to begin a card for each child in his own classes and has no guarantee that anyone will continue the records when the child leaves his class. In one year, the teacher can accumulate sufficient facts and assessments to enable him to make an evaluation of the child's progress which would be reliable and which could also be of benefit to the child.

It is undoubtedly true that a teacher who does this is letting himself in for much additional work. But it is also true that teachers generally are willing to undertake anything which will improve the value of the education a child is receiving. Advances in educational methods have invariably come about through the efforts, in the

155

P. Lafitte and N. F. Holt

first place, of teachers who were enthusiastic and willing to apply new ideas to their work.[1]

Conclusion

It has been implied that the enthusiastic teacher who is concerned with the progress of a child, rather than with the task of teaching a given subject, will use examinations to give information that will help him in his work and the child in his development. This pupil-centred attitude requires that a class should learn to regard and accept examinations as practical and necessary aids to learning, as ways of discovering something about oneself.

Each question, and the examinations as a whole, should be designed to discover, for both partners in the teaching process, what the child knows, what he does not know, and why he does not. The last question then becomes the starting point for an individual exercise in educational guidance.

SELECTED REFERENCES FOR FURTHER READING

1. CAMPBELL, H. M., 'Mathematics as a Training for Reasoning', in: *Mathematics in the Secondary School* (Australian Council for Educational Research, Melbourne University Press, 1940, pp. 15–31). Discusses the usefulness of mathematics for training in clear thinking and illustrates with several examples for classroom use.
2. BRERETON, J. L., *The Case for Examinations* (London, Cambridge University Press, 1944). A critical, important study of the place of examinations in education, its purpose being to show that they are an essential part of the machinery of education.
3. KANDEL, I. L., *Examinations and their Substitutes in the United States* (New York, Merrymount Press, 1936). Traces the history of the development of the present examining methods in the U.S.A. and reviews in detail the criticisms of older methods and the achievements of new types of tests.
4. HARTOG, SIR PHILIP, RHODES, E. C. and BURT, SIR CYRIL, *The Marks of Examiners* (London, Macmillan, 1936). A statistical comparison of the marks given in a number of secondary and tertiary examinations in England by many independent examiners.
5. New Education Fellowship, *The Examination Tangle and the Way Out* (London, Shenval Press, 1935). A readable account of most of the debatable aspects of examination practices, without complicated statistical argument.

---

[1] See reference No. 3 for a detailed discussion of the structure of Cumulative Record Cards used in some schools in the U.S.A.

The Purpose and Conduct of Examinations

6. VALENTINE, C. W., *The Reliability of Examinations* (University of London Press, 1933). A report of an inquiry extending over several years into the usefulness of examinations, particularly for selecting students for secondary schools and universities.
7. *Secondary Education: A Report of the Advisory Council on Education in Scotland* (Edinburgh, H.M.S.O., 1947). A review of the whole of secondary education in Scotland. It concludes a concise, readable chapter on examinations and methods of marking them.

X

Educational and Vocational Guidance

A. R. GREIG

Synopsis

So far, this book has dealt with the major phases of a teacher's work: getting motivation to learn, teaching the skills of citizenship, adjusting himself to his own roles, helping children to adjust within the classroom so that they can function fully within the limits of their abilities.

But the teacher is also concerned with what happens to his pupils when they leave his care. The following chapter discusses some of the important aspects of educational and vocational guidance with which the teacher is concerned, and in which he can help his pupils to face and to make a transition to the problems and responsibilities of their adult work roles.

Introduction

Guidance has popularly been thought of as fitting people to jobs by using a battery of tests. Young people, in conflict over the choice of a career, consult a vocational guidance expert and expect that he will be able to tell them exactly what job they will be best at and happiest in. They are often disappointed when, after tests and interviews, he indicates some broad areas of the total job field to which they appear best suited, other areas in which it appears likely that they will not succeed or be satisfied, explains how they can find out more about the particular jobs in these areas, and leaves them to make their own decision.

Vocational guidance is only one aspect of what the psychologist means by guidance. In its broadest sense it means every kind of psychological advice, counselling and assistance. Everyone may, at some time or other, require such guidance. The young child requires guidance most of the time. As he grows older he normally becomes more independent, more able to guide himself, but at any stage in life even the most mature person may require expert advice and guidance of some kind. Many who are less mature and well adjusted, require guidance all through their lives. Furthermore, most people are only too ready to hand out information and advice on any matter at all. Some of this information is accurate and useful, but there is no doubt that some of it is also inaccurate, and may be seriously misleading.

One aim of the scientist is to find out by experiment more about the phenomena of the field in which he is working so that such knowledge may be used in guiding others in this field. The field of the science of psychology is human behaviour. One of the most important branches of study is the study of social behaviour; and psychological guidance, in its broadest sense, aims at using all the knowledge gained by the experimental psychologist to help individuals and groups in their attempts to adapt to the society in which they live. The more complex society becomes, the more necessary it becomes to place guidance on a scientific basis in order to reduce the incidence of social maladjustment.

It may be said then, that 'ideally conceived, guidance enables each individual to understand his abilities and interests, to develop them as well as possible, to relate them to life goals and finally to reach a state of complete and mature self-guidance as a desirable citizen of a democratic social order'(1).

Guidance always involves the adjustment of the whole person to his total environmental situation. If any aspect of the person's total personality and physical make-up, particularly the strong social needs discussed in earlier chapters, or any aspect of the total environmental situation are neglected, guidance will be incomplete and possibly misleading. This is true whether the guidance takes place at school and is called Educational Guidance, or later in the child's school career when it is called Pre-vocational Guidance, or later still, at the end of his schooling, when it is called Vocational Guidance. The statement is also true when the guidance is concerned with the more serious forms of social maladjustment and is carried out in a psychological or psychiatric clinic. These subdivisions of guidance are thus in a sense artificial, as each subdivision includes all the others to a greater or less degree.

Educational and pre-vocational guidance are best carried out at school, as part of the educational process and with the full and active co-operation of teachers.

The Cumulative Record Card

In the previous chapter, cumulative record cards were briefly mentioned. It is proposed to consider them now in greater detail.

The first essential of any form of guidance is a detailed and accurate case history. Obviously, the school guidance officer must have as much information about the person as possible. The best case history is one which begins at the time the child enters kindergarten and continues to accumulate information in a form that is both convenient and meaningful, during the whole of the child's school career. Such cumulative case histories are recorded on what is generally known as a cumulative record card. A carefully designed and accurately used cumulative record card can be the basis for a sound guidance programme. It is also of great value to the teacher in his daily contact with the child.

For such records to be of value to the teacher or psychologist they must be accurately entered and kept up to date. The initial entries are made when the child enters the school, and it is very important that such standard information as name, address, age, father's and mother's occupations be accurately entered in the first place and checked by each new grade teacher. Entering test results and evaluating them is a task for the psychologist in conjunction with the class teacher. Clerical help may also be desirable.

Valuable information about the child's social adjustment and school achievement can be obtained from the class teacher. He has more contact with the child than anyone else in the school situation, and with care can usually make useful assessments of the child's

160

adjustment in class, in organized games, and at play. He may also obtain useful information about home background, an important matter for dealing with problem children. He can note, for instance, the aggressive child, the bully, the anti-social child, or the nervous, timid, shy child, and such symptoms of tension as stammering, facial twitches and excessive blinking, nail biting, thumb-sucking, and so on. He can also note the socially well-adjusted child and the potential leader. Useful methods of noting such behaviour trends and common indications of maladjustment have been discussed in detail in chapters 7 and 8.

The class teacher is also, of course, in a position to assess the child's progress in the various school subjects in relation to that of the rest of the class. Such assessments, considered in relation to standardized achievement tests and tests of general ability, are the basis for predictions of future academic attainment.

Although any one teacher, because of lack of insight or prejudice, may misjudge a child on any of the above aspects of adjustment as the child passes from grade to grade and school to school, the impressions of different teachers in each successive year, faithfully recorded, together with results from tests and examinations, will provide an accumulation of evidence on the basis of which sound guidance can be given.

Accumulated case histories of this kind are of great value to the teacher. They assist in grading his class or form, in sub-dividing it into smaller groups, as discussed in the chapter on classroom motivation, in attempting to understand the particular problems and difficulties of individual children, in discussing the child's adjustment and school progress with his parents, the head teacher or inspectors, in referring the child for special medical or psychological examination, and in discussing with guidance officer, head teacher, and parents, the problems of guidance into post-primary schools or vocations.

Cumulative records require time and effort to compile; but their value to the class-teacher, the head teacher, the guidance officer, the psychologist, the psychiatrist, or any other agency with which the child comes into contact for the purpose of helping him to make an adequate adjustment to his social group, make them well worth the effort.

A. R. Greig

It should be realized, however, that unless they are carefully designed and conscientiously kept, record cards may be seriously misleading. Record cards which require many subjective judgments to be made—for instance the assessment of personality traits by unqualified people—or that have been carelessly kept by a staff member are worse than useless.

Educational Guidance

In so far as it is possible to separate educational guidance from other forms of guidance, it may be considered as being concerned with the problems associated with the optimal adjustment of the child to the school situation. Educational guidance will, therefore, be more important in the early part of the child's school life. As he approaches school leaving age his adjustment problems become more and more those connected with training for and placement in a job, and become the subject of prevocational and vocational guidance.

'Mental Age' and 'Readiness'

Children are at present admitted to school and often promoted by chronological age only. The child of six with a Binet I.Q. of 50 has the intellectual maturity of an average child (I.Q. 100) of three. The child of six with an I.Q. of 125 on the Binet scale has the same intellectual capacity as the average child of seven and a half years. Should all these children be put into the same grade and given the same material to learn in the same way? Obviously not. Only about 33 per cent. of the total population have I.Q.'s between 95 and 105 and thus mental ages that approximate their chronological ages. For the rest—for 66 per cent. of our school populations—the practice of taking chronological age only into account leads to the kind of discrepancy illustrated above.

A child's readiness to begin any kind of learning is a function of his maturity, and this should be assessed by appropriate tests.

Testing in this field is a relatively recent development. The type of test used is designed to give a measure of the child's readiness to learn a particular subject. Although these tests have particular value for indicating a child's readiness to begin formal schooling, the

162

concept can be extended to measure readiness to learn at any new level. This approach has interesting implications for curriculum research, but this is not the place to deal with them.

The Problem of Discrepancy Between Ability and Attainment

Children who, on the basis of tests of general ability, standardized attainment tests, and school performance, are achieving considerably below their ability level in any subject, require:

(i) full psychological and physical examination to diagnose the cause of such retardation, followed by suitable treatment:

(ii) remedial teaching in the subjects concerned.

The discrepancy may be due to physical causes such as illness, accident, poor hearing or eyesight that have remained undetected, too many changes of school, poor teaching, etc. More often, however, a discrepancy between ability and attainment is due to emotional disturbances caused by social maladjustment. If this is the case—and elimination of other possible causes will often indicate this—full investigation, diagnosis, and treatment is essential if the child is to make satisfactory social adjustment and educational progress at this stage or in the future.

Such maladjustment may, of course, give rise to many other symptoms as well as to educational backwardness. These symptoms, and the methods of psychological investigation and treatment used to relieve them, have been discussed in the chapter on Problem Children. The possible contribution of the school and the teacher to their prevention and cure is also discussed in the chapter on Classroom Motivation.

Pre-vocational Guidance

At the stage where the primary school population begins to split into the various post-primary streams, each with its own vocational bias, children and their parents need pre-vocational guidance.

The post-primary streaming occurs at different ages and with different degrees of rigidity in the various educational systems of the world.

In some educational systems the first change occurs at eleven-plus years. The several kinds of post-primary schools available are each orientated toward a certain segment of the vocational field

A. R. Greig

and once the original decision has been made it is often difficult to transfer from one to another of these post-primary schools.

In attempting guidance from this stage onward, not only ability levels as measured by tests and general motivation toward learning must be considered, but also those special kinds of motivation usually referred to as vocational interests.

Now an interest in a certain kind of job or job group presupposes some knowledge of that job or job group. Present-day industry is extremely complex and one must ask: What knowledge of the main aspects of the job field has the young boy or girl of eleven to twelve years of age on which to base a sound, realistic vocational interest even in the broadest sense, and what knowledge have his parents with which to guide him?

In order to obtain reliable data on the basis of job interests, a carefully planned investigation was carried out in 1949 on Form III boys of a Melbourne Technical School (4).

Information was obtained from psychological tests, mid-year examination results, questionnaires from pupils and their parents, essays on expected jobs by students, and interviews of selected students.

The results of this investigation indicate that although all Form III students make important decisions regarding their future vocations before next year, less than six months before that time:

(a) Approximately 20 per cent (n = 22) have no idea what job they will go into or begin training for next year.

(b) All of the remaining 80 per cent have chosen jobs. (Nine of these choices for various reasons were not the student's first preference.) But of this group of ninety-five pupils:

(i) not more than 12 per cent have made job choices based on adequate knowledge of the job they intend to take;

(ii) not more than 50 per cent have abilities commensurate with their job choice;

(iii) the abilities of 20 per cent are inadequate and the abilities of 15 per cent more are of doubtful adequacy for success in their chosen job;

(iv) the abilities of 15 per cent are much higher than success in their chosen job requires.

164

Educational and Vocational Guidance

(c) Although parents respect their children's interests—and none in this sample would force a child into a job that he did not like—very few showed any indication that they realized how inaccurate and unreal were the grounds upon which the interests of their children rested. Few parents understood the relation between abilities and success in a vocation.

Many parents showed marked concern with the problem of finding a suitable job for their son and the indications are that they would welcome expert assistance in this direction.

It appears, then, that the bases upon which Form III students in Melbourne Technical Schools (and probably all Victorian Technical Schools) and their parents at present make decisions about future education and occupation are grossly inadequate, and that in many cases such decisions are not likely to lead to vocational placements that are in the best interests of the individual student (4).

Most essays of these boys on a day's work in their chosen job reveal an almost complete lack of knowledge and a large degree of fantasy.

These results, it should be stressed, are from Form III pupils whose average age was fourteen and a half years, and who had had the vocational experience and training of nearly three years in a Technical School. On what basis did these students decide, two and a half years earlier, to go to the Technical School rather than the High School?

If the grounds upon which third year pupils in Technical Schools make job choices are 'grossly inadequate', then it seems certain that the grounds upon which Grade VI pupils in Primary Schools decide between Technical and High Schools are yet more inadequate.

Available tests appear to be of little value in differentiating between probable success in the various post-primary school courses. Also, the other main criterion of differentiation, the child's vocational interests, are at this stage quite immature and unstable, and there are no means of predicting the trend of their future development. Thus, sound guidance at this level is, to say the least, extremely difficult.

Many educational authorities are aware of this. They defer pre-vocational streaming until considerably later, and provide a broad curriculum which includes a variety of practical subjects.

A. R. Greig

Because of the great complexity of modern industry and the instability of the interests of young children, it appears that the older a child is when he has to make such a choice the better. However, when this stage is reached—and all children and their parents must sooner or later make such decisions—there is no doubt that a comprehensive guidance service is the best safeguard against unsound decisions and consequent later educational, social, and vocational maladjustment that can be provided at present.

However, having decided on a post-primary school, a student has taken only the first step in preparing for and entering on a career. As he progresses through post-primary school he must make further decisions regarding courses and subjects that become more and more specific to a certain chosen vocation. A comprehensive guidance programme is thus also necessary in all post-primary schools if educational and vocational maladjustment with their serious consequences to both the individual and society are to be reduced to a minimum.

Guidance in Post-primary Schools

To provide guidance, in the broadest sense of the word, to all pupils in post-primary schools, would entail:

(*a*) Taking over and carrying further the cumulative record cards from the primary school.

(*b*) Interviews at regular intervals as well as at any time the pupil feels the need for one, and close contact with the class teachers to obtain the information discussed in the section on cumulative record cards. During these interviews the child's interest trends would be carefully investigated and he would be given advice and encouragement to find out more about his job interests. Carefully worded questionnaires for students and parents and perhaps an essay on the child's preferred job would give valuable information as well as opportunities for discussion, particularly as regards the degree of fantasy involved in his job choice.

(*c*) A close watch should be kept on the child's adjustment to his new school, particularly during the early part of the first year and, when necessary, notes on this should be entered in the cumulative record card. The sort of behaviour, social adjustment, and school progress that can reasonably be expected can be determined from

166

his primary school record, and any marked discrepancy between this and the child's actual progress should be investigated as a probable symptom of his failure to adjust adequately to the new school.

In some educational systems, the change from primary to post-primary school is rather sudden. The child finds himself in a strange situation amongst strangers of whom he is one of the smallest and knows the least. The school is large and many subjects are new to him. The teachers are strangers and come and go from period to period so that he seldom gets to know any of them, nor do they get to know him. Most children can undergo this with a minimum of disturbance; but to some, particularly the shy, timid, introverted child, the bad mixer who shows as an isolate on the sociogram (see Chapter 5), it can be a traumatic experience, and can seriously affect his behaviour and school progress.

Such children require assistance. A friendly chat with an understanding form master may suffice, but often more is needed, and in some cases the assistance of a psychologist or psychiatrist will be required. Neglect of these cases may lead to more serious problems later and many cases of truancy, delinquency, problem behaviour in school, failure to adjust in the playground, lack of school progress, neurotic symptoms, and a desire to leave school at the first opportunity, could be prevented if these early signs of failure to adjust were recognized and referred to trained specialists.

We may look upon the change from primary to post-primary school as something of a test of the child's social adjustment. It is likely to aggravate any personality weaknesses that exist. Children who have trouble in making this adjustment, then, require assistance and therapy, and a very important aspect of guidance in post-primary schools consists of recognizing these children and helping them in whatever ways appear necessary and possible.

(*d*) At certain stages in his post-primary school life the child must make further pre-vocational decisions. He must decide between certain alternative courses or groups of subjects. For instance, in Victoria in Form III of High School, children may take a Commercial or a Professional course, and later they must decide between certain groups of subjects for Leaving and Matriculation courses. In Form III of Technical Schools the child must decide between a

A. R. Greig

professional course leading on to a Technical Diploma or several Trade Intermediate courses. Or he may leave school at fourteen and must then decide on a vocation.

Each of these courses leads to a different job group, and it is very important that such decisions be made on a sound basis.

The child should be prepared for making such decisions by a carefully planned programme aimed at supplying a maximum amount of job information in a form that is both meaningful and reliable. This will help him to build up stable and realistic job interests. Talks by guidance officers, specialist teachers, and industrialists are all helpful. They should be of a general nature and aimed at stimulating interest and investigation in the early years, but should become more specific to the main job groups later. Such talks should be supplemented by motion pictures and visits to typical factories where possible. Carefully prepared pamphlets on all main job groups should be available to students in later forms and students should feel free to come and discuss any problem related to job choice with the guidance officer (counsellor) or teachers at any time.

In some instances vocational information classes have become part of the normal school curriculum (5). In Victorian Junior Technical Schools the vocational information classes are seen as the most important aspect of the whole guidance programme. These classes aim to help the student to clarify his vocational interests by introducing him to the vocational field and its main sub-divisions, by discussion of the work done in the main jobs open to him, and then by the use of the Rothwell Interest Blank which effectively highlights his vocational interests and dislikes. This is followed by a closer study (preferably by a vocational guidance project) of the group of jobs in which he shows the strongest interest with the aim of finally selecting the occupation that appears most suitable in all respects.

It is of course at the critical or change points in the child's school career that he and his parents most require guidance, and interviews with the guidance officer should be given at suitable times for this purpose. One or both of the child's parents should be present at these interviews when possible.

Preliminary information regarding the child's job interests and the parents' desires may be obtained by means of interest inventories or questionnaires, and this, in conjunction with the information already on the child's cumulative record card, should give the teacher or guidance officer a fairly comprehensive picture of the problems before the interview begins.

Where a Vocational Information course is operating and each student has carefully considered all aspects of the most likely alternative jobs in his vocational guidance project, the main purpose of the interview at this stage is to examine the validity of his decision (arrived at via the project), point out further problems, misconceptions and confusions and give further information as required (5).

When the decision is to leave school and begin work, the guidance officer, who should be in contact with local industry, may suggest placements that in his opinion appear suitable and he often arranges for the child to interview the firms concerned.

The cumulative record at this stage would contain information on abilities, achievements, social adjustments, and interest from the primary school. From the post-primary school it would contain records of all interviews, interest trends, further notes on social adjustment and attitudes to education, examination results and the results of tests of general abilities, special aptitudes and attainments. Opinions formed during a single interview may be inaccurate, the assessment of any one teacher or guidance officer or test may be biased and misleading. But a carefully compiled cumulative record card contains the opinions of many teachers and of several guidance officers together with the results of many tests and school examinations.

At the interview, the school counsellor or guidance officer places before the child and his parents, in a simple and meaningful form, all relevant information regarding the child and the job groups in which he is interested. He points out the advantages and disadvantages, the possible alternatives, the difficulties and the prospects of the various courses of action that appear suitable. *The final decision must always rest with the child and his parents.*

Students doing senior courses in secondary schools, senior technical schools, and many studying for university degrees also require guidance in various ways. Apart from educational and vocational problems—such as the student who is failing in examinations, or the one whose interests are changing and who is no longer

A. R. Greig

sure that he wants to continue with his course—this age group often presents emotional problems of early adolescence which may cause serious disturbance to school progress and social adjustment. This again emphasizes the need to recognize the symptoms of maladjustment and to take the necessary therapeutic steps as discussed in the chapter on the problem child.

In schools which provide a variety of evening courses, some form of guidance appears to be necessary to ensure that pupils taking these courses are fully aware of their uses and limitations, of their difficulty, level and length, and thus of their chances of attaining whatever goal they have in mind in attempting such courses.

A close liaison should also be maintained between the schools guidance service and all other social agencies dealing with child and youth welfare and with industrial selection or placement.

Finally, guidance officers in post-primary schools should conduct follow-up studies in an attempt to assess the validity of the guidance procedures used. Only in this way can any guidance programme be evaluated and its shortcomings discovered and rectified.

Such a programme of testing, test evaluation, interviewing of children, teachers, parents, and industrialists, evaluation of personality factors and adjustment problems, and giving advice to students, parents, and teachers on all aspects of educational, social, and vocational adjustment, should be carried out by psychologists who are also trained and experienced teachers. They will, of course, need the co-operation and understanding of the staffs of the schools in which they work. Working together and with the aid of the other specialists, the clinical psychologist, psychiatrist, and physician, the teachers and the guidance officer can reach a high level of efficiency in guiding the child through his school years and on through adolescence to function as a well-adjusted adult member of society.

SELECTED REFERENCES FOR FURTHER READING

1. TRAXLER, E. T., *Techniques of Guidance* (New York, Harper, 1945). This is a useful and reliable textbook giving a comprehensive treatment of the fundamental principles and techniques of educational and vocational guidance including the design and uses of cumulative records, testing, interviewing and counselling.

Educational and Vocational Guidance

2. SUPER, D. E., *Appraising Vocational Fitness* (New York, Harper, 1949). This book aims to provide the user of vocational tests with a detailed and objective appraisal of the value of a large number of widely used tests and other techniques of guidance. The book also brings together and interprets the results of research with existing tests and attempts to familiarize the reader with bibliographical sources in order that he may be in a position to keep abreast of research developments in the field.

3. WOOLF, M. D., and WOOLF, J. A., *The Student Personnel Program* (New York, McGraw-Hill, 1953). This text presents an extremely comprehensive programme of student personnel work at secondary and tertiary levels. It brings together many and varied phases of personnel work such as orientation of new students, counselling, citizenship training, self government, group processes and therapy, and a new and positive approach to problems of discipline and describes the processes of co-ordination and integration of personnel services into the school system.

4. GREIG, A. R., 'A Study of Job Expectations and Preferences of Form III Students in Victorian Technical Schools', *Austral. J. Psychol.*, **2**, 1950, 80–89. This brief study, carried out prior to the introduction of vocational guidance into Victorian Technical Schools, shows clearly the need for such a service by exposing the discrepancies between the nature of the work the entrance and training, requirements, etc., for the jobs students had chosen and the students' actual knowledge of these important factors.

5. HOPPOCK, R., *Group Guidance* (New York, McGraw-Hill, 1949). This book has been written as a general guide for the counsellor or teacher in organizing a scheme of group guidance. It discusses, in a very practical manner, every aspect of the problem such as its place in the school programme, what it should attempt to cover, and who should teach it. It goes on to discuss and evaluate various techniques that the author has tried out over a period of years, and finishes with a useful evaluation of the important researches in this field.

Appendix to Chapter 10

THE CUMULATIVE RECORD CARD

THERE are innumerable types of cumulative record forms. That on pp. 174-5 is an illustration of one which is well laid out and easy to use. It was designed for Forms I–IV of a secondary school. The instructions for its use are also given. Without careful instructions which can be followed by successive form masters, record cards can be very misleading.

The form a cumulative record card should take, the information it should contain, the methods by which that information is obtained and recorded and the use to which it is put, will depend upon such aspects of the school concerned as its educational level (primary, secondary, tertiary), the variety of courses offered, the points at which students must make important decisions regarding their future education and occupation, the training and experience of the personnel who will compile and use the material recorded, and the amount of time at their disposal for this purpose.

The cumulative record card shown below was developed for use in secondary schools offering a four-year course from twelve years of age. At the end of the third year about 70 per cent. of the students leave school and enter employment. The remainder have a choice of courses for Form IV and can then either enter employment or begin tertiary courses at the end of Form IV.

The guidance is carried out by teacher careers-advisers who devote at least half of their time to this work. The careers-advisers are not trained as psychologists but are supervised and assisted as necessary by qualified educational psychologists.

EDUCATIONAL AND VOCATIONAL GUIDANCE
CUMULATIVE RECORD CARD

INSTRUCTIONS

THIS Cumulative Record Card is designed for use in secondary schools. It should contain, in a readily accessible and concise form, all available information about a pupil relevant to educational and vocational guidance at any stage of his progress through the school. This will include information about his home background, his school progress, any peculiarities of physique, school or social adjustment relevant to educational and vocational guidance, his general and special abilities as indicated by standardized tests and a record of information obtained and decisions reached in all interviews between the child, his parents, teachers, and the careers-adviser.

The purpose of keeping Cumulative Records is:

1. To provide accumulating information about each pupil to be used in discussions between the pupil, his parents, teachers, and careers-adviser for the purpose of making educational and/or vocational plans, especially at the end of Forms III and IV.
2. To provide information about pupils who present symptoms of psychological maladjustment. This record is not intended to contain a case-history sufficiently detailed and reliable for diagnostic or therapeutic purposes. It should, however, contain sufficient information about all pupils, their problems, school progress, ability levels and home background to indicate which ones require specialist attention, and will provide the psychologist with some useful information from which to proceed.
3. To assist teachers in such matters as: getting acquainted with pupils at the beginning of each school year, dividing classes into sub-groups, recognizing very bright or dull pupils, gaining a better understanding of individual pupils who are having unusual difficulty with any aspect of school work.
4. To assist teachers to make careful, systematic judgments.

MALE/FEMALE

.............SECONDARY SCHOOL

SECONDARY SCHOOL PERSONAL RECORD CARD

				DATE OF BIRTH		PREVIOUS SCHOOL	
1	NAME					ADDRESS	PHONE

	FAMILY DETAILS	AGE	EDUCATION	OCCUPATION	HEALTH	COMMENTS ON FAMILY BACKGROUND
2	FATHER					
3	MOTHER					
4	SIBLINGS					

		19	19	19	19	19	COMMENTS ON ADJUSTMENT
5	YEAR						
6	Physique and Health						
7	School Adjustment						
8	Social Adjustment						
9	ATTENDANCE						

		Mid Year	Final	Mid Year	Final	Mid Year	Final	Mid Year	Final	Mid Year	Final	COMMENTS ON SCHOOL PROGRESS
10	FORM											
11	AGE (at 1st Jan.)											
12	Accel. or Retard											
13	Exam. Results											
14	Place in Class											
15	Number in Class											
16	Average % Marks											
17	Certificates Gained											

	PSYCHOLOGICAL TESTS			TEST PROFILE	COMMENTS ON TEST PERFORMANCE
18	DATE	TYPE AND TITLE OF TEST	R.S.	RATING	

174

	Initials	Date
21 SUMMARY AND DECISIONS—FORMS I—III		
22 EDUCATIONAL AND VOCATIONAL PLANS OF CHILD AND PARENTS—FORM IV		
23 SUMMARY AND DECISIONS—FORM IV		

A. R. Greig

Filling in the Record Cards

The careers-adviser will be responsible for filling in, checking, keeping up to date, and filing the record cards. These cards will contain much confidential information; and whilst they should always be readily accessible to teachers, it will be the responsibility of the careers-adviser to keep them in safe custody, to supervise their use by other teachers and, when necessary, to interpret to other teachers the information they contain.

The cards should be raised early in Form I year and entered in accordance with the following guide:

Cross out Male or Female as appropriate. Before the heading 'Secondary School' enter the name of the school. After the heading 'Previous School' enter the name of the school last attended by the pupil.

1. *Pupil's name, Date of Birth, Address, Telephone Number.*
Enter surname first in block capitals, then full Christian names. Address and telephone number should be checked at regular intervals and any changes entered.

2. 3. 4. *Family Data*
Enter full names of father, mother (or guardian), and siblings, the education they have received, present occupation and relevant comments on their health. If parents are living apart this should be noted and the address of both parents obtained if possible. The main purpose of this section is to estimate the probable influence of the pupil's home background on his educational and vocational ambitions, plans, prospects, and opportunities. Any necessary additional notes should be entered under 'Comments on Family Background' *and dated.*

5.–12. *School Record*
Entries will be made in sections 5–12 for each year the child is at the school. Four columns are provided for the normal four-year course and an extra column for pupils who spend two years in any one form.
Entries in sections 6–7–8 will be made only when the child's behaviour is sufficiently atypical to interfere with his satisfactory educational progress or social or vocational adjustment.

6. *Physique and Health*

This information should be obtained from physical education or medical records when these are available, otherwise it must be obtained by careful questioning and discussion with the pupil and when necessary his parents. The following important conditions should be checked:

(a) Size: If unusually big, small, strong, or weak.

(b) Disabilities: Physical deformities as loss of leg, arm, hand, fingers, eyes; flat feet or other foot disability, lameness, hernia, spasticity, stutter, stammer or other speech defect, poor eyesight or hearing, colour blindness.

(c) Serious Illnesses: Asthma, epilepsy, heart disease, rheumatic fever, poliomyelitis, rickets, skin diseases, St. Vitus Dance (chorea), tuberculosis, etc.

If any of the above conditions exist further details as to present condition and future prognosis should be obtained from parents, physical education teacher, or medical officer, entered under 'Comments on Adjustment'(*with the date*), and duly considered when discussing future educational and vocational plans with pupil and parents. If none of the above conditions exist in sufficient degree to influence educational progress or vocational efficiency a tick should be entered in the appropriate space.

7. *School Adjustment*

This heading refers to the pupil's classroom behaviour. Marked aggression and hostility to teachers and/or other pupils; extreme timidity and nervousness, lack of interest, or inability to concentrate are the main symptoms of classroom maladjustment met with. This space should be ticked unless there are clear signs of such maladjustment.

8. *Social Adjustment*

This heading refers to the pupil's peer relationships, mainly his adjustment in the playground and in organized sport. As with 7 above, the space should be ticked unless there are clear signs of maladjustment. The child who is a persistent playground bully or in any way extremely aggressive in play or organized sport, the nervous timid child who takes no part in such activities, or the child who is rejected by his fellows should be noted under

177

A. R. Greig

this heading and any necessary details added under 'Comments on Adjustment' and dated.

9. *Attendance.*
Here again the space should be ticked unless attendance is such as to interfere with school progress or unless the pupil has been truant. The reasons for poor attendance should be entered under 'Comments on Adjustment' and dated. Entries under sections 7 and 8 and some under section 9 will usually indicate that a pupil's maladjustment is such as to warrant referral for further psychological investigation and treatment. When such a referral is made, details should be entered under 'Comments on Adjustment' and dated. Details of the outcome of such treatment should also be entered as they become available.

10. Enter Form and section for each year.

11. Enter age on 1st January each year.

12. Enter acceleration or retardation in months using + to indicate acceleration and — to indicate retardation, thus:

$+ \dfrac{9}{12}$ i.e. the pupil is 9 months younger than the average for his form, indicates an acceleration of 9 months; while

$- \dfrac{9}{12}$ i.e. the pupil is 9 months older than the average for his form, indicates retardation of 9 months.

Acceleration or retardation of less than 6 months should be ignored.

13–17. This section should present, in summary, the pupil's progress in each half-year through Forms I to IV. A space for comments on school progress is provided and any factor requiring investigation, such as weakness in particular subjects, a sudden deterioration in examination results in some or all subjects, or any information relevant to vocational choice such as apparent differential ability (i.e. strong in practical subjects, weak in Maths., etc.) should be entered under 'Comments on School Progress' and dated. Details of examination results are available from the school examination records.

178

Educational and Vocational Guidance

18. Enter results of standardized tests as indicated by column headings. The full titles of tests used should be entered, as without this, meaningful interpretation of results is impossible. Intelligence test results should be entered as a raw score. Standardized 'band' ratings rather than I.Q. grade norms are most suitable for attainment tests. The results should also be marked on the accompanying Test Profile. Any comments regarding behaviour, conditions of health, etc., in the test situation or peculiarities of test performance should be entered under 'Comments on Test Performance' opposite the test concerned.

19. Enter the subject's full name, surname first, in block capitals followed by full Christian names.

20. *Educational and Vocational Plans of Child and Parents—Forms I—III*

    During Form III year, or earlier in the case of pupils intending to leave school before they reach this level, further information will be obtained from the following sources.

    (a) Questionnaire to parents asking about their wishes for the pupil's further education and occupation.
    (b) Interest inventory from pupil to indicate major areas of vocational interest.

    This information and any relevant information from sections 2–18 should be entered in summary form in this section.

    This space may also be used to enter brief notes on interviews and discussions with the student and any other aspect of his school adjustment, work in vocational information classes, vocational plans and their level of reality, hobbies, work, experience, etc., as thought necessary from Forms I–III. All entries in this section must be initialled by the interviewer *and dated.*

21. *Summary and Decision Forms I–III*

    The pupil, and whenever possible his parents, will be interviewed during the latter part of Form III year or earlier if the pupil is leaving school, when all the above information will be fully discussed and an attempt made to arrive at a decision regarding the child's future education and/or vocation that appears to be most consistent with all that is known about him at this stage.

A. R. Greig

Brief notes on this interview and the decision arrived at should be entered in this section, initialled and dated by the interviewer.

22. 23. These sections will be used for pupils in Form IV in the same way as described above for Form I–III under sections 20 and 21.

Again, all entries must be initialled and dated by interviewer.

Appendix

Refresher School in Psychology for Teachers
Report of Proceedings

O. A. OESER

Preface

THE purpose of including this report is, first, to show one example of the way in which the contents of this book could be used for intensive refresher course. Each teacher of educational psychology would handle the assignment differently, depending on his interests, resources, and audience. Secondly it illustrates the use of group methods, which in this particular case appeared to have been strikingly successful: the intensity of learning and of participation were high; and, more important, there was cogent evidence that the great majority of participants reported considerable changes in their attitudes to teaching, to children, and to psychology.

Introduction

The Refresher Schools' Co-ordinating Committee of the School of Education asked the Department of Psychology at Melbourne University to run a Refresher School in Psychology. This was welcomed as a good opportunity for discussing some recent developments in social psychology that have a bearing on practical teaching, and for studying attitude changes in teachers.

O. A. Oeser

The first problem was to limit the field to what could reasonably be presented and discussed in three days, since there is almost no branch of psychology that has not some relevance to the theory and practice of teaching.

It was decided to treat subjects of general importance to all teachers, whether in primary, secondary, technical, or special schools, and to omit subjects that are adequately treated in most textbooks. This meant leaving out methods of teaching specified subjects, the theory of intelligence and intelligence testing, the psychology of learning and perception, manual and verbal skills, and child development.

The theme of the course was then set on the following considerations: Psychologically speaking no one can be taught anything unless that person wants to learn or, as the modern textbooks say, is 'motivated'. Without adequate motivation only rote learning is possible on the part of the pupil, and rote teaching or drill on the part of the teacher.

If one starts with the problem of motivation, certain other major problems faced by all teachers fall into place. First, the problems of the teacher in the classroom: classroom discipline, judging character and personality, establishing motivation or desire to learn. Secondly, the problems of children in the classroom: education for citizenship, the peer group and its functions. And, thirdly, the problem child, who is a problem to himself, his parents, and his teacher.

Summary of Proceedings

Monday, 22nd May

Introductory remarks were concerned with the problem of motivation. The problem of teaching from the teacher's point of view is the same as the problem of learning from the pupil's point of view, being fundamentally one of motivation and not of methods of teaching of learning any given subject. If the motivation is present in the right strength, learning follows as a matter of course. Only after the learning process has started can the efficiency of learning be improved by refinements in the methods of teaching. One of the tasks of the course was to investigate the origin of two sharply different attitudes of children to school. Children attending some

182

schools are angry when they have to stay at home through illness, whereas other children are delighted.

The second purpose was put in this way: The course would not attempt to tell teachers much that is new about the behaviour of children, but would try to help them to analyse and classify their knowledge and to relate it to the theories of modern social psychology.

One of the difficulties facing teachers is that they must act all the time, administer rolls, instruct, ask questions, keep discipline, mark papers, fill in forms. There is little time for reflection and generalization about their behaviour. Consequently, a teacher is largely forced to act on implicit popular assumptions, such as that a child who does not concentrate is a child who will not concentrate, and that the solution is to urge or impel the child to concentrate.

But perhaps the most important aspect of the Refresher School was that the group leaders did not set out to *teach* or *instruct*. Instead the conference was broken up into groups of between sixteen and eighteen persons, who by active participation were expected to *learn* something about the principles of learning in a group setting.

In order to provide material from the teacher's own experience for the theme of the first day—classroom discipline—an opinion poll was carried out concerning appropriate action to be taken in fourteen common situations in the classroom, e.g. a child lacks concentration, a boy bullies smaller children, a child is noisy while working, and so on.

A full analysis of the answers to this questionnaire would take up far too much space here. Suffice it to say that 70 per cent of the answers revealed autocratic ways of dealing with such situations, and only 30 per cent democratic or therapeutic. Though there were differences between primary and secondary schools and between State and non-State schools, these differences were statistically not significant.

As a further preparation for intensive group discussion, the first part of the film *Classroom Discipline* was shown. As soon as the film had been shown the audience dispersed to fifteen separate classrooms.

Outline of the work groups programme. The first step was for the group leader to introduce himself and to get every member of the group in turn to introduce himself, to state briefly how many years' teaching experience he had had, what he taught in what types and sizes of schools. This introductory or settling-down period was followed by a discussion of the problems raised by the film.

Stage 2 was designed to take discussions out of the abstract sphere of principles and textbook knowledge and to set the stage for discussion at a reality level. For this the method of role playing was used. Essentially this consists in two or sometimes more people dramatizing some incident, e.g. 'a teacher speaks to a girl who makes too much noise in class', 'a head teacher addresses a noisy class in the absence of the class teacher', 'the teacher deals with a child caught cheating'.

After lunch the second part of the film was shown. The first part had told the story of an ordinary old-fashioned kind of classroom and teacher. The second part showed how the same teacher by changing his attitude to the children and to the teaching process produced striking changes in the relations both of children to himself and to each other.

Further material was provided for the groups by summaries from recent literature in social psychology (see references). The groups were now led to draw conclusions from their discussions through the following stages:

(i) the group leader sets the goal;
(ii) the problem is formulated and proposals made;
(iii) the stage of information seeking and giving (note that group leaders had been instructed to resist attempts to extract authoritative information from them, since their role was not to be teachers but group discussion leaders);
(iv) the stage of proposals for solution;
(v) the stage of developing proposals, further discussion, further information seeking and giving, opposing and supporting;
(vi) the stage of summarizing and formulating.

This group learning technique was thought of in terms of four phases that should be followed in any teaching sequence of this kind. Firstly, the expectation was shaken that the group leader's role would be to teach or instruct. Secondly, the group was provided with shared experiences (questionnaire, film, summaries of articles and directed discussion). Thirdly, these two devices should have created an atmosphere of inter-personal friendliness, objectivity and motivation to observe, communicate, and learn. Fourthly, the group situation should have provided practice in role playing and non-directed discussion. The aim of these four phases is through experience of this group process to direct the attitude of teachers to their own classroom procedures.

The concluding lecture was concerned with the question 'Why does the problem of discipline arise?' Certain goals have been set (learning English, mathematics, etc.) and the problem of the teacher is to generate interest and motivation, so that these goals may be reached. The needs that operate in a classroom are not biological needs but social ones. These social needs, it is true, cannot show themselves until biological needs have been satisfied, i.e. a starving child cannot be taught. But once the biological needs have been satisfied the social needs also fall into a hierarchy, and it is part of the teacher's job to find out the nature of the hierarchy and the strength of each social need. A young child clearly can feel little need to learn arithmetic. The motivation on which the learning of arithmetic must be based is therefore to be sought in other needs, such as acceptance by the teacher, acceptance by the group, need for co-operative activities.

The commonest motivations in teaching are competition—that is aggression between individuals—and fear: fear of punishment, and fear of disapproval by authority (the teacher or the parents). The commonest incentives are marks of approval. These incentives are indirect and very little is done in ordinary classroom practice to substitute direct incentives springing from the desire to communicate and co-operate with one's fellows.

Put in another way, the goals of classroom teaching remain remote until the child is old enough to understand these goals. This usually does not happen until somewhere around the Leaving Certificate stage. Goals such as learning to spell and do arithmetic are certainly connected with the activities of adults, but they lie in the future and bear little relation to the child's immediate biological and social needs. That is possibly the most important reason why a collection of children in the classroom presents problems of discipline. The relation between ends and means must be such that it is not too remote, can be apprehended by the child, can be within its powers, and can satisfy a need. When ends and means are in the process of being related the child is said to be motivated.

The lecture went on to discuss the relation between discipline or control and initiative, with particular reference to the study of Lippitt and White on social climates in the classroom. With too much control there is too little initiative. Without control initiative is apt to seek the wrong goals. Without initiative there is stagnation and the teacher is again forced into autocratic methods of driving children. The best form of control is by means of a set of rules that are accepted by a group, and where this happens, as in a team game, discipline is exercised through the acceptance of group goals and rules of conduct, and only an occasional individual has to be punished. In society, control is exercised in this way. The classroom, however, in most schools has no social structure, being entirely teacher-centred. There are consequently few outlets for aggressive impulses and equally few outlets for creative impulses. The social impulses for relationship between individuals are almost completely blocked.

The lecture illustrated that, except for rote learning, none of the following achieve adequate motivation for learning: authoritarian atmosphere, threats, corporal punishment, individualist competition, teacher-oriented lessons. The article of Coch and French was abstracted to show that the principles outlined above are applicable not only to teaching but to industrial relations as well. In other words, the principles of social psychology in their general form are applicable to all human relations, of which the relations in the classroom are merely an example. On the other hand, motivation is achieved by permissive atmospheres, by building up group belongingness through work groups, by task-oriented teaching, and by inter-group competition in small doses for the purpose of setting standards.

This discussion of the relation between needs, control, and discipline, and between ends and means led over into the second day, which was to be concerned with the problems of judging personality and with the perception of personality as part of a total social context.

Tuesday, 23rd May

The introductory lecture outlined some of the problems of judging character and personality. The discussions and role-playing

of the previous day had helped considerably to make clearer the
different roles that teachers have to play in the classroom, and the
lecture was concerned with distinguishing between social roles and
personality characteristics, in particular with the fact that the personality of the child is viewed quite differently by the teacher according to the particular role he happens unconsciously to adopt. These
points were illustrated by three examples:

(i) judgments about vocational aptitude of a thousand school-
leavers in a Scottish school system. In this example, the judgments of the teacher became more and more inefficient the
further removed the role was from what the teacher usually
conceived it to be;
(ii) teachers' reports to parents drawn from some schools in
Victoria, which showed that the child is generally regarded in
isolation and that a problem, such as laziness, is laid at the
child's door and no attempt is made to see it as the result of
circumstances both within and outside the classroom;
(iii) ratings of personality characteristics as expressed in behaviour problems made by teachers and by mental hygiene
experts. Briefly, teachers rate transgressions against authority
and dishonesty near the top of the scale of behaviour problems and withdrawn recessive behaviour near the bottom,
whereas mental hygiene experts reverse these ratings.

The general theme of personality was then taken up and discussion
centred on contextual analysis: personality is a social product and
traits such as honesty and loyalty are specific to certain situations.
This is true also of the important concept of leadership.

Leadership arises out of a social context and the leader will change
according as the task which has to be faced by the group changes. In
the normal classroom situation, pupils are denied opportunities for
social leadership and initiative. The major influences on the pupil are
not, as is usually assumed, from the teacher, but from his peer group.
Investigations show that on the whole the teacher is rejected in all
classes in which teaching method is based on authoritarian and
hierarchical procedures. The teacher's attitude, nevertheless, is of
very great importance to the development of personality structure,
particularly in the forming of attitudes towards authority. Various

O. A. Oeser

techniques, such as rating scales and the explicit formulation of roles as a preliminary to any personality judgments, were discussed. Judgments of personality are always made in a context, and it is necessary for the teacher to consider all available evidence in the appropriate order.

These themes were taken up by the work groups and discussed further on the basis of literature summaries (Asch, MacFarlane, Anderson, Keister). Topics for role playing were designed to bring out various factors in teacher-parent relations. The work groups performed a simple experiment which showed that judgments of personality can be very different in different verbal contexts, and then proceeded to a close study of the Moreno sociometric method.

This is in essence a very simple device by means of which the teacher can rapidly gain insight into the social links that exist between the children in the classroom. The use of the sociometric diagram was discussed from its practical aspects: to make it possible for the teacher so to group the children in a classroom that maximum inter-personal relations and stimulation become possible. The group leaders gave examples of the application of this method at different ages and for different teaching purposes, and the discussion centred on the problems of discipline and levels of aspiration, already raised on the first day. Sociometric methods also show clearly what children are isolates, that is, have no social relations with the other children in the class, and this served as a link to the next day, when the problem child was to be discussed.

The afternoon summing-up centred mainly on the problem of adolescence. The main reason why adolescence is a period of problems both for the child and the teacher is that the rights and privileges of adulthood are withheld for as long as possible in our particular culture pattern. Comparison with other cultures shows quite clearly that whether or not adolescence presents problems depends on this crucial factor. In Australia, the adolescent is kept within various rigid patterns of behaviour, and these, though they have social sanction, often have no psychological justification from the point of view of the adolescent.

Further consideration of the concept of maladjustment was designed to lead into discussion of problem children on the third day. In an important sense, the word 'maladjustment' is a misnomer. An

188

individual adjusts to the social psychological circumstances in which he finds himself. The way in which he adjusts gives us insight into his perception of the world, in particular the existence of what he perceives to be permissive situations, on the one hand, and hostile or repressive situations on the other. Therefore, the problem which has to be solved before a child can be adjusted to a different perception of the world, more in keeping with that generally accepted, is to find out the symbolic structure of his perceptions.

Wednesday, 24th May

The introductory remarks were concerned with a review of the problems that are faced by all children in the classroom and with the special case of the 'problem child'. Many studies have shown that the teacher pays far too much attention to the cognitive problems faced by the child (i.e. how to solve this particular mathematical puzzle, or write an essay) and far too little to the emotional problems faced by a child in his relations to the teacher, to the social climate of the classroom, and in his relations to other children. An example of the way in which emotional problems affect a child's cognitive attitudes is that there is a high correlation between liking a subject and liking the teacher of that subject.

Special attention was paid to the isolate, the child who has no friends either inside or outside the class. It was shown that isolation in turn is strongly related to the kind and amount of tensions in the family. The difference between class captains chosen by the teacher and the 'ring-leaders' chosen by the children was also illustrated.

These various problems again throw light on the underlying motivational structure and the relation of intellectual interests to general social relations between child and teacher and other children.

'The problem child' was taken up next. Case studies were used to illustrate methods for approaching the readjustment of the problem child in a general way, by changing the seating, using the sociogram to help the child become identified with a small social group, by remedial teaching, and by contact with the parents. To provide material for further discussion by the work groups, a film *Learning to Understand Children* was shown. The groups then settled down to work through some case histories. The discussions were summarized under the headings of 'The problems which a child faces in the classroom', 'What is the function of the teacher in solving them?', 'What is a problem child?', 'How does one recognize a problem child?', and 'What steps does one take to seek for a solution?'.

A further task for the work groups on this day was the formulation of sets of recommendations for changing teaching practice. The final lecture summed up the discussions of the three days. First, the evidence against the still widely held doctrine of 'formal discipline' was reviewed. The evidence comes from everyday observation, physiology and brain anatomy, and psychological experiments. In particular, the development of social psychology has drawn attention to the selective forces which operate in the formation of personality and to the fact that social factors such as co-operativeness, which are necessary for the smooth functioning of society as a whole, are given very little opportunity to develop in schools in which teaching is task or teacher centred, and the individual during the learning process is isolated from his peer group.

The key problem in motivation is to establish harmonious relations within the classroom. Once this key problem has been recognized, functionally related problems fall into place: the relation between discipline and authority, and between discipline and control, the relation between working out problems co-operatively in a group and the need for individual thinking and initiative.

This same set of problems was illustrated from a different point of view by considering the difference between co-education and co-instruction.

Finally, it was shown that by confining life in the classroom to the intellectual level the school plays almost no part in training for citizenship; but that classroom teaching based on group work, the inter-relations between children themselves, and the spontaneous emergence of leaders, makes teaching approximate to a psychological guidance process which should operate throughout a child's school life.

Addendum

The groups were each asked to work out an agreed statement about what they had learnt and what suggestions they could make for future courses. In addition, many individual teachers wrote brief comments.

Appendix

These comments and statements of some 250 participants would take up too much space, even in a highly condensed and summarized version. To readers of this report who did not participate, such a summary would be relatively meaningless. However, three major conclusions were practically unanimous:

1. Participants found (sometimes to their surprise) that they had worked extremely hard, yet had not had enough time for discussion although there had been only two lectures a day. They agreed that one reason—perhaps the chief reason—was that their motivation and interest had been aroused by the method of working in groups; and that they would therefore try this method out in their classrooms.

2. Their attitudes to the teacher's role and to the social dynamics of the classroom had been considerably modified. (One went so far as to write 'It made one ashamed of past misdemeanours!')

3. Several resolutions demanded more information, and more help from the School of Education and the Department of Psychology in gaining insight into the human problems faced daily by teachers.

To implement these resolutions the group leaders met again and in several long sessions constructed the outlines for this book.

REFERENCES

ANDERSON, H. H., 'Dominative and Socially Integrative Behaviour' in, Barker, Kounin, and Wright (eds.), *Child Behaviour and Development* (New York, McGraw-Hill, 1943).

ASCH, S. E., 'Forming Impressions of Personality', *J. Abn. Soc. Psychol.*, 41, 1946.

BURT, C., *The Backward Child* (University of London Press, 1946).

COCH., L., and FRENCH, J. R. P., 'Overcoming Resistance to Change', *Hum. Rel.*, 1, No. 4, 1949.

COOPER, D., 'The Potentialities of Sociometry for School Administration', *J. Sociom.*, 1947.

DEUTSCH, MORTON, 'An Experimental Study of the Effects of Co-operation and Competition upon Group Processes', *Hum. Rel.*, 2, No. 2, 1949.

FLEMING, C. M., *Adolescence, Its Social Psychology* (London, Routledge & Kegan Paul, 1948).

LIPPITT, R., and WHITE, R. K., 'An Experimental Study of Leadership and Group Life', in Newcomb and Hartley (eds.), *Readings in Social Psychology* (New York, Holt, 1947)

O. A. Oeser

THELEN, H. A., and WITHALL, J., 'Three Frames of Reference, The Description of Climate', *Hum. Rel.*, **2**, No. 2, 1949.

The following are chapters in: BARKER, KOUNIN and WRIGHT (eds.), *Child Behaviour and Development* (New York, McGraw-Hill, 1943).

KEISTER, M. E., 'The Behaviour of Young Children in Failure'.

LIPPITT, R., and WHITE, R. K., 'The "Social Climate" of Children's Groups'.

MACFARLANE, J. W., 'Study of Personality Development'.

Index

Ability and attainment, discrepant, 163
  and group formation, 89, 93
  and test results, 119–21
Acceleration, in promotion, 129
Acceptance, social, and learning, 9, 10
Achievement, and group methods, 102
Active learning, 54
Activity, importance of, 10
Activity areas, school, 6–7
Adaptation, local, of curricula, 28
Adjustment, school and home, 82
Adolescence, 188
  sociometry and, 81–2
Adult living, development towards, 27–8
Adult society, teacher as representing, 22–3
Age, mental, 109, 162
Analyst, social, teacher as, 22
Anderson, H. H., 47, 191
Anxiety, 40, 42, 102
Arithmetic, and group methods, 102
Asch, S. E., 191
Attention seekers, 137
Authority, acceptance on, 51
  attitudes to, 2
  education and, 6
Authority figure, teacher as, 7

Baby-talk, 136
Backwardness, educational, 129–130
  mental, 127–8
'Bad' children, 45–6
Barker, Kounin, and Wright, 47, 192
Barton Hall, M., 141
Bavelas, A., and Lewin, K., 48
Behaviour, pupil and teacher views of, 8–9
  right, 6

Benjamin, J., 47
Benjamin, Z., 142
Best, R. J., 63
Billinglea, F. Y., and Bloom, H., 49
Bonney, M. E., 49, 80, 85
Boredom, 105
Bowley, A. H., 142
Bradford, Benne, and Lippitt, 29
Brereton, J. L., 146, 152, 156
Bright children, 128–9
Brown, Francis J., 18, 29
Bühler, C., and others, 142
Burt, C., 191
Burton, W. H., 25
Buxbaum, E., 142

Campbell, H. M., 156
Carmichael, L., 48, 123
Catell, R. B., 123
Child, I. L., and Whiting, W. M., 48
Child, needs of, 39 ff
Citizenship, 64
Clarification, 13
Classroom, 37
  physical set-up, 95–6
  pupil's view of, 41 ff
  social structure of, 50 ff
  teacher's view of, 38
Cleugh, M. F., 142
Cliques, 51
Coch, L., and French, J. R. P., 47, 186, 191
Communication, 9, 14
Concentration, 14
Conformity, 37
Consultant, teacher as, 54
Cooper, D., 191
Co-operation, staff, 21
Counsellor, teacher as, 23

Index

Cramming, 147
Crying, 40
Culture patterns, transmission of, 34
Curriculum, child-centred methods and, 24 ff
   subject-matter and experience, 26–7
Curry, W. B., 16

Deafness, 138–9
Deformities, 138–9
Democracy, 15–16
Democratic atmosphere, 100
Desks, 95
Deutsch, M., 48, 61, 63, 191
Discipline, formal, 2–3, 190
   maintenance of, 23
Discussion, 52
   group, 55
Dyslalia, 136

Efficiency, in classroom situation, 58–9
Emotion, and learning, 9
Emotional behaviour, abnormal, 131
   development, 101–2
English, and group methods, 99
Enuresis, 137–8
Errors, in intelligence tests, 111
   in achievement tests, 117
Examinations, 103–4, 115–16, 144 ff
   class, 147
   disadvantages, 145–6
   frequent, 147
   relevance in, 148
   reliability, 149–51
   uses of, 145
   wording of questions, 148
Experience units, 26–7
Expert, teacher as, 23–4
Expression, oral, 101
   personal, 42

Family background and behaviour, 34–5, 46
Fleming, C. M., 191
Frankel, E. B., 77, 84–5
Freedom, use of, 94–5
Freud, Sigmund, 14
Friends, placement of, 91–2
Friendship, 80
Frustration, 105

Goal, need of understanding, 15
Goal-setting, 43 ff
Goals, remote and substitute, 9, 43
Goodenough, F., 123
Greig, A. R., 171
Group methods, advantages, 100
   outcomes, 100 ff
Group teaching, suitable subjects, 88
Groups, in classroom, 12, 50 ff, 87 ff
   criteria, for forming, 88–9, 93
   friendship, 37–8, 41
   methods of formation, 93 ff
Guidance, 158 ff
   educational, 162 ff
   in post-primary schools, 166 ff
   pre-vocational, 163 ff
   for senior pupils, 169–70
   vocational, 158–9

Harriman, P. L., 47–8
Hartog, Sir P., and others, 156
Hearing aids, 138–9
Heart, learning by, 3
Hierarchy, among teachers, 19–20
Hoppock, R., 171
Hostility, repressed, 33
Human qualities, and learning, 3
Hymes, J. L., 142

Inattentiveness, 131–2
Incentives, 31–2, 43, 185
Individual attention, 130
Indulgence, parental, 35
Initiative, 186
Insecure child, 40–1
Intelligence quotient, 110
Intelligence tests, see Tests
Interaction, pupil, 9
   teacher-pupil, 52 ff
Interest, how sustained, 3
Interviews, 166, 169
Isolates, 66 ff, 81
   aggressive and recessive, 81
   and group formation, 89–90
   in nursery schools, 79

Jenkins, G. G., and others, 142
Jennings, H. H., 81, 85
Job interests, 164, 168

Index

Jones, H. E., 123
Jones, V., 48

Kandel, I. L., 147, 156
Kelly, H. H., 63
Kesister, M. E., 192
Krech, D., and Critchfield, R. S., 48

Laziness, 5, 131–2
Leadership, 50, 60, 187
  sociometry and, 81
Lecture, 52
Lecture-discussion, 52–3
Left-handedness, 139–40
Lewin, K., 48, 49, 63, 92
Lighting, classroom, 96
Lippitt, R., and White, R. K., 44, 47, 186, 191, 192
Lisping, 40
Love, 13
Lying, 133–5

McCarthy, D., 48
MacFarlane, J. W., 192
Maladjustment, 188–9
Marking, in examinations, 151–2
Marks, 61
Masturbation, 137–8
Methodologist, teacher as, 24
Miles, C. C., 123
Moreno, J. L., 67, 83, 84
Moss, H. A., 47
Motivation, 9–10, 31 ff, 42 ff, 182–3, 185
Murphy, Murphy, and Newcomb, 49

Need satisfaction, 32–4
Needs, conflict of, 42–3
  social and physical, 32–3
Newcomb, T. M., and Hartley, G. L., 48
Norms, test, 109, 116
Northway, Mary L., 67, 84
Nursery school children, relationships, 76–7
Nurses, 3

Oeser, O. A., 63
Oeser, O. A., and Emery, F. E., 16

Oeser, O. A., and Hammond, S. B., 16, 63
Ottaway, A. K. C., 16
Overprotection, parental, 35

Parents, teacher's attitude to 4–5
Passive learning, 52–3
Personality, 18–19, 101
Personality traits, sociometry and, 80 ff
'Pet, teacher's', 36
Physical defects, 138–9
'Platoon systems', 92–3
Plodders, 127–8
Post-primary school, adjustment to, 140, 167
Potashin, R., 80, 85
Pressure, parental, 128, 129–30
Preston, M. G., and Heintz, R. K., 47
Problem cases, reference to specialists 140
Problem child, 124 ff, 189
  definition, 125
Problems, classification, 126
Psychometrics, 12
Psychoneuroses, 140
Psychosis, 140
Punishment, 7, 10, 34, 40, 46
Pupils, teacher's relations with, 5 ff

Quick children, 128–9

Radio project, 96–8
Ranges, age and ability, 126–7
Rapport, 112
Readiness, 162–3
Reading, and tests, 122
Records, cumulative, 155, 160–2, 166, 169, 172–80
Refresher course, 181 ff
Regression, 42
Rejected child, 90–1
Relationships, inter-class, 64 ff
Retardation, in promotion, 129
Rewards, 7, 34
Ridenour, N., and Johnson, I., 142–3
Riesman, D., 62, 63
Rothwell Interest Blank, 168
Russell, Bertrand (Lord), 15

Index

Schonnel, F. J., 118, 123
School, importance of society in, 2
School-leaving, early, reasons for, 9
Schwebel, M., and Asch, M. J., 48
Seating, class-room, 95–6
Self-esteem, 34–7
Seminar, 55
Sight, weak, 139
Snygg, D., and Combs, A. W., 29, 46
Social skills, 101
Social studies, grouping for, 89
Sociogram, 73 ff
Sociomatrix, 71–3
Sociometry, 12, 64 ff, 188
Speech disorders, 136–7
Stammering, 136–7
Status, professional, teacher's, 20–1
   social, development, 79 ff
Stealing, 132–3
Stephenson, W., 123
Streader, D. C., 46
Study course, development of, 28–9
Subculture, represented by teacher, 22
Super, D. E. 171
Suttie, I. D., 48
Syndicate, 55

Tact, 12
Teacher, needs of, 38
   professional relations, 4, 18, **19** ff
   relations with pupils, 5 ff, 19
   roles of, 4 ff, 18 ff
Teagarden, F. M., 143
Tele, 66
Tensions, 44
   removal of, 12

Terman, L. M., and Merrill, M. A., 123
Tester, teacher as, 113
Tests, coaching and, 115
   defective children and, 114
   illness and, 114
   "objective", 153–4
   psychological, 105 ff; achievement, 107, 115 ff; aptitude, 106–7; diagnostic, 107, 115, 118–19; group, 107, 112; intelligence, 106, 107 ff; kinds, 106–7; reason for, 105–6; value of, 110–12
   of readiness, 163
   schooling and, 114–15
   sociometric, 67, 83
   use for group formation, 93–4
   use of results, 119–21
   young children and, 114
   see also Examinations
Thelen, H. A., and Withall, J., 47, 192
Thumb-sucking, 40
Time-sampling, 76–7
Transfer, of training, 3
Traxler, E. T., 170
Truancy, 135–6

Under-production, 44

Valentine, C. W., 157
Vernon, P. E., 123
Vocational information classes, 168

Webb, L. W., 16
Wechsler, D., 123
Withal, J., 49
Woolf, M. D., and J. A., 171